Young
POETRY CO

GREAT MINDS

Your World...Your Future...YOUR WORDS

From The Midlands Vol II
Edited by Steve Twelvetree

Young Writers

First published in Great Britain in 2005 by:
Young Writers
Remus House
Coltsfoot Drive
Peterborough
PE2 9JX
Telephone: 01733 890066
Website: www.youngwriters.co.uk

All Rights Reserved

© Copyright Contributors 2005

SB ISBN 1 84602 084 0

Foreword

This year, the Young Writers' 'Great Minds' competition proudly presents a showcase of the best poetic talent selected from over 40,000 up-and-coming writers nationwide.

Young Writers was established in 1991 to promote the reading and writing of poetry within schools and to the youth of today. Our books nurture and inspire confidence in the ability of young writers and provide a snapshot of poems written in schools and at home by budding poets of the future.

The thought, effort, imagination and hard work put into each poem impressed us all and the task of selecting poems was a difficult but nevertheless enjoyable experience.

We hope you are as pleased as we are with the final selection and that you and your family continue to be entertained with *Great Minds From The Midlands Vol II* for many years to come.

Contents

Georgina Price (13)	1

Ellesmere College, Ellesmere
Paddy Fuller (11)	1
Hugh Wignall (11)	2
Ross Tattersall (11)	2
Alexander Owen (11)	3
Henry Cureton (12)	3
Charles Gbadmosi (11)	4
Zoë Evans (12)	4
Melissa Evans (12)	5
James Leahy (11)	5
Lauren Stevenson (11)	6
Natasha Taylor (12)	6
Charlotte Shearer (11)	7
Rosie Rickett (11)	8
Samantha Wolfson (12)	9

Garibaldi College, Mansfield
Marcus Birkin (11)	9
Jack Parnwell (13)	10
Rebecca Holloway (11)	10
Victoria Gelsthorpe (11)	11
Sarah Chandler (13)	11
Daniel Jones (13)	12
Thomas Helmkay (13)	12
Tanisha Guy (14)	13
Grant Davidson (11)	13
Liane Powell (11)	14
Zoe Godfrey (11)	14
Natalie Swain (13)	15
Paige Matthews (11)	15
Amy Gillespie (13)	16
Conor Boothey	17
James Allsopp (13)	18
Kristie Wathall (11)	18
Alexander Gibson (13)	19
Holly Brailsford (11)	19

Zoey Marples (13)	20
William Hall (11)	20
Frances Woolley (13)	21
Abbey Haynes (11)	21
Danni Rushby (13)	22
Dean Haywood (11)	22
Joe Hessey (13)	23
Laura Baxter (13)	23
Rachael Hammond (14)	24
Jessica Towns (13)	24
Alix Waddell (13)	25
Niall Haslam (13)	25
Callum Charity (13)	26
Kayleigh Marshall (13)	26
Corey Alvey (13)	27
Tom Waddingham (13)	27
Matthew Hollis (13)	28
Kirsten Tackie (13)	28

Highfields School, Matlock

Sam Waterfall (13)	29
Connor Boyes (13)	29
Faye Kilburn (16)	30
Ceri Thorpe (16)	31
Thomas Crowder (12)	32
Chris Wayne (12)	32
Rachel Quinn (12)	33
Dale Travis (12)	34

Malvern College, Malvern

Tom Knowles (13)	34
Leo Manibhandu (14)	35
Bob Stirling (13)	35
Lily Sanders (13)	36
Lucille Perry (14)	37
Robert Killick (14)	38
Sarah Stilliard (14)	38
William Bishop (13)	39
Ayobami Afolabi	39

Quince Tree School, Tamworth
    Brian Hanslow (16)   40
    Adam Burd (16)   40
    Brett Jennings (16)   41
    Stephen Baker (16)   41
    Craig Berrow (18)   42
    Georgina Unwin (17)   42
    Lee Goodfellow (16)   43
    Donna Allen (17)   43
    Samantha McIntyre (16)   44

Retford Oaks High School, Retford
    Tom Newby (13)   44
    Emma Woollard (13)   45
    Ellie Whitmore (13)   45
    Kelli Beech (13)   46
    Charlotte Kelly (13)   47
    Charlotte Kent (13)   48
    Katie Meads (13)   48
    Kyle Chapman (13)   49
    Bethany White (11)   49
    Joe McFarlane (11)   49
    Stuart Payling (13)   50
    Elanor Kerr (14)   50
    Sarah Hargreaves (14)   51
    Donna Tong (14)   51

Sutton Centre Community College, Sutton-in-Ashfield
    Amber Severn (12)   52
    Rachel Scholes (12)   53
    Jessica Beardall (12)   54
    Richard Clayton (12)   54
    Amy Taylor (12)   55
    Melanie Cudworth (11)   55
    Heidi Fellows (12)   56
    Hayley Buck (11)   56
    Francesca Brooks (12)   57
    Sharni Cross (11)   57
    Catherine Geraghty (12)   58
    Melissa Burton (13)   59
    Josie Raffan (12)   60

Kirsty Parnill (12)	61
Rachel Fox (11)	62
Natalie Maskell (11)	62
Joshuah Alik Goncearenko (11)	63
Kimberly Barsby (11)	63
Elizabeth Whiley (12)	64
Laura Whittingham (12)	65
Daniel Warren (13)	66
Natasha Donbayand (11)	66
Mark Sanders (12)	67
Jade Hagan (11)	67
Coral Depledge (13)	68
Nicola Shaw (11)	68
Emma Wass (12)	69
John Wadley (12)	69
Marc Baumanis (12)	70
Michael Smith (12)	70
Meg Whawell (12)	71

The Holgate Comprehensive School, Hucknall

Paige Whitehead (13)	72
Phil Dearden (12)	72
Grace Carpenter (13)	73
Emma Mooken (12)	73
Charlie Pates (11)	74
Amber Curtis (12)	74
Brenn Burbanks (11)	75
Anthony Burnell (11)	75
Callum Urquhart (13)	76
Victoria Bamford (11)	76
Louise Colton (13)	77
Emma Maddox (11)	77
Reece Foster (12)	78
Aimee Hadman (11)	78
Niall Christie (13)	79
Macha Haskey (13)	79
Liam Hunter (13)	80
Rosie Richardson (13)	80
Sarra England (13)	81
Jamie Hufton (11)	81
Daniela Mabbott (14)	82

Harry Share (12)   83
Anya Smith (12)   84
Kyle Winfield (11)   84
Kyle Thomas (12)   85
Daniel Bullin (11)   85
Louise Bailey (15)   86
Lauri Jo Dennis (12)   86
Fraser Pearson (13)   87
Octavia Wisbey (12)   87
Natalie Arme (14)   88
Katie Hough (12)   88
Holly Spencer (12)   89
Daniel Evans (11)   89
Hannah McConnell (12)   90
Simon Greensmith (13)   90
Dale Cotterill (13)   91
Megan Lynch (11)   91
Kyle Lester (13)   92
Jessica Wheatley (12)   93
Matt Clifton (12)   94
Ellis Gormley (12)   95
Rebecca Thorley (12)   96
Toni French (14)   96
Travis Prew (13)   97

The Lakelands School, Ellesmere
Adrian Dean (11)   97
Jackie Jones (11)   98
William Martin (11)   99
Henry Traynor (12)   100
Joe Hatton (11)   100
Becky Jeffrey (12)   101
Louise Norris (11)   102

The Long Eaton School, Long Eaton
Katie Freeman (14)   102
Rachel Sloper (12)   103
Gemma Pickering (13)   103
Josh Allsop (13)   104
Jemma Shaw (13)   104
Abby Mycroft (13)   105

Matthew Debbage (14)	105
Holly Kemish (13)	106
Laura Codrington (12)	106
Emma Riley (14)	107
Craig White (13)	107
Catherine McLaughlin (14)	108
Katie Clayton (12)	108
James Glover (14)	109
Amy Platkiw (13)	109
Jade Sheppard (14)	110
Siân Groves (13)	111
Michelle Newbold (13)	112
Scott Twells (13)	112
Robert Porter (12)	113
Serena Metcalfe (13)	113
Brittany Woodhouse (12)	114
Sarah Francis (12)	114
Ryan Walker (12)	115
Ashley Matthews (13)	115
Anna Smith (14)	116
Tom Gatehouse (12)	117
Callum Whaley (13)	118
Sophie Hesketh (12)	118

The Marches School, Oswestry

Angus Martin (16)	119
Alex Winfield (16)	120
Robert Manning (15)	121

The Priory School, Shrewsbury

Georgina Blay (14)	122
Scott Peever (15)	122
Harriet Dineen (14)	123
Katie Brearley (14)	123
Daniel Pugh (14)	124
Charles Andrews (13)	124
Joseph Sadowski (14)	125
Zoe Davies (15)	125
Becky Lea (15)	126
Olivia Rossall (13)	127
Megan Evans (12)	128

Andy Cormack (14)	129
Joe Travis (12)	130
Grace Thompson (13)	130
Holly Edwards (13)	131
Emily Bidder (13)	131
Natalie Watkins (12)	132
Kelly Beesty (13)	132
Heather Manger (12)	133
Hannah Gorski (12)	133
Will Jones (13)	134
Suzy Marrs (13)	135
Amy Wyatt (12)	136
Sana Ayub (11)	137
James Fisher (12)	138
Fred Woollaston (11)	138
Emma Neen (13)	139
Rosemary Evans (13)	139
Rachel Meyrick (12)	140
Lucy Jennings (12)	141
Nikki Allcock (13)	142
Hannah Wilson (15)	143
Gareth Thomas (16)	144
Chloe Fletcher (12)	145
James Holmes (15)	146
Chris Barber (13)	146
Sarah Lee (15)	147
Rachael Randall (15)	147
Claire Doyle (15)	148
Becky Taylor (12)	149
Adam Redman (15)	150
Lucy Balcombe (13)	150
Emma Lea (12)	151
Becki Crawford (13)	151
Edward Trethowan (15)	152
Robert Pritchard (16)	153
Tori Pearson (11)	154
Olivia Hewings (13)	155
Maya Garrett (14)	156
Becky Seward (12)	157
Michael Beeston (14)	158
Laura Davies (13)	158
Sarah Cox (14)	159

Ciara Merrick (13)	159
Eloise Jackson (13)	160
Mia Tivey (13)	161
Neal Tomlinson (14)	162
Amy Templeton (13)	163
Emma Jane Harris (13)	164
Becky Bruce (13)	165
Alex Drake-Wilson (13)	166
Ellie Quinlan (14)	167
Andrew Chebsey (13)	168
Tom Davies (13)	169
Jasmin Bayliss (15)	170
Camilla Clay (13)	170
Ashleigh Bennett (13)	171
Rachel Benson (14)	171
Georgina Minton (13)	172
Simon Stallard (13)	172
Emma Hunt (13)	173
Madeline Watkins (13)	173
Rosanna Franklin (13)	174
Charlotte Harrison (14)	175
Christopher Shaw (16)	176
Abby Quinlan (15)	176
Matt Harrison (14)	177
Kaytie Evans-Jones (11)	177
Amy Harrison (15)	178
Alex O'Fee-Worth (11)	179
Bethany Thomas (11)	180
Alex Emberton (11)	180
Megan Rose Reece (11)	181
Rosie Coxhead (11)	181
Georgina Thomas (14)	182
Matthew Edwards (11)	182
Lucie Short (11)	183
Melissa Amy Morris (11)	183
Hayley Steadman (14)	184
Holly Ashford (14)	185
Jennifer Smyth (11)	186
Danielle Dodd (11)	187

The Poems

Excalibur

Beyond the lush green meadow lay a lake
As deep and still as 'twere a silver sea.
And Arthur, lord and king of all who spake,
Took himself unto the rushy shore
And found a boat and into it he stepp'd
And by the ripples from the shore was kept.

Then suddenly rose forth an arm in silken sheen
Which in its slender fingers did hold out
A sword of rarest beauty every seen;
Its hilt was gold and set about with jewels
With sapphires fair as any summer's day
And rubies red as blood - a bright array.

The blade was of the truest, keenest steel
And silver as a moonbeam in the night.
Then Arthur in his heart of hearts did feel
That he, as king, should take it as his own.
And so he lean'd and took the sword from her;
In awe he grasp'd the sword, Excalibur.

Georgina Price (13)

My Terrifying Teacher

My terrifying teacher
Her name is Mrs Crackpot
A staple gun,
A hammer and masonry nails in her desk.
My terrifying teacher
Penetrating blue eyes
She most likely has razor-sharp teeth,
At tin of poisoned sweets.
My terrifying teacher
Silver bullets, steel stakes
I doubt any of these will even hurt
My terrifying teacher!

Paddy Fuller (11)
Ellesmere College, Ellesmere

The Swinger

Look in the trees,
There's a swinger
With bees,
As he
Feels a mighty sting.

He yelps out in pain,
As he's stung through
The brain,
And he falls
With a *splat* on the
Ground.

He wears a linen cloth,
He raises his hands
In the air,
When
Suddenly:
'George come out
Of the garden, it's
Time for lunch!'

Hugh Wignall (11)
Ellesmere College, Ellesmere

Bullseye

I pull the bowstring back,
Like I'm going to attack,
I stop when it's at my chin,
I really want to win!

I hold it for a pose,
My knees are shaking, so are my toes,
I finally let it go,
It hits the target and then they say, *'Wow!'*

Ross Tattersall (11)
Ellesmere College, Ellesmere

My Mazda RX8

My Mazda RX8.
Is really comfortable and great.
When it has my dad's load,
It can really hog the road.

The rotary engine
Builds up the tension.
It roars like a lion,
When you set the accelerator 'flying'.

The air conditioner is so strong,
It will freeze you before long.
When it is in full flow,
It's really hard to slow.

When you're feeling great,
Nothing can stop the Mazda RX8.

Alexander Owen (11)
Ellesmere College, Ellesmere

Horror On TV

It's dusk; I'm watching horror on TV,
My adrenalin is high.
I'm hoping I'm not next to die!

I love horrors!
They make my mind go wild,
The screaming and shouting
The cold mist rising into fog.

When the horror has finished
I stare at the TV screen
Wondering what to do next . . .

I scare myself silly,
Watching horror on TV!

Henry Cureton (12)
Ellesmere College, Ellesmere

My Brother Stinks!

My brother stinks!
All he does is eat, sleep and drink.
After he goes to the toilet
He does not wash his hands at the sink.
My brother stinks.

My brother is dirty with grit
He has home-made sleeping gas under his armpit.
He has manure and mud all over his games kit.
My brother is dirty with grit.

My brother smells really bad.
The way he lounges about drives me mad.
He does it to everyone, even my dad
My brother smells really bad.

My brother is mad!

Charles Gbadmosi (11)
Ellesmere College, Ellesmere

Books

Books sit on a shelf
Leaning and squashing each other,
A bit like a scrum in rugby,
They're like thousands of people
All squashed in a tiny room.
They just sit there and occasionally flutter
In the passing wind,
They always look so very lonely,
The most exciting thing that happens
Is when they fall from the shelf!
Still that only happens about once a year.
They feel free as soon as someone opens them,
But a book will be a book and that's what they will do,
Just sit, in a row, until one of them is removed.

Zoë Evans (12)
Ellesmere College, Ellesmere

Excuses, Excuses!

'Miss, I haven't done my homework!
I was too busy watching horror,
I took an hour eating dinner,
I promise to do it tomorrow,
And it will be a winner!'

'Miss, I haven't done my homework!
I know . . . it's the second time running,
I was catching kittens,
And being really cunning.
I promise to do it tomorrow,
And it'll be a winner!'

'Miss, I haven't done my homework!
I know it's the third time,
I was busy watching the clouds,
They were moving in a straight line!
I promise to do it tomorrow . . .
And it'll be a . . . *no!*'

Melissa Evans (12)
Ellesmere College, Ellesmere

Sit And Wait

I sit and wait,
I don't know what for,
I observe the beautiful landscape.
I wonder why,
The rolling hills are there,
The divine trees, standing upright,
Then rain begins to fall,
I don't mind,
The cold or the wet,
I'll do anything as long as I can see,
The beautiful landscape in front of me.

James Leahy (11)
Ellesmere College, Ellesmere

White Cloud

He stands so proud,
My friend White Cloud,
He has the grace of a swan
As he soars through the air,
The courage of a lion
Because he has no fear,
He big brown eyes,
Bright and alert,
Every stride solid,
So as not to get hurt.
He never falters,
He never sways,
Fantastic clear round!
We finish the course,
Oh my magnificent, beautiful horse.

Lauren Stevenson (11)
Ellesmere College, Ellesmere

Black Stallion

My brave steed
Rears up against the night,
Protects me from my fright.
As the night goes on,
He battles on
Gently through the night.

As I open my eyes
To my surprise,
He gallops on,
Into the sun.
That brave, black horse
That I adore,
Goes on through the night.

Natasha Taylor (12)
Ellesmere College, Ellesmere

Boo!

There's something around me
I don't know what.
I'm scared to death,
What could it be?

It might be a robber.
Or a big wild cat,
They may have my mum
Or even my dad.

I worry about them,
My mum's not that strong.
They could have been killed,
Oh no!

There's a knock at the door,
I whisper, 'Is there anyone there?'
They're out to get me but
Nobody cares.

I hug the covers over my head,
Crying out to the night.
I wonder what is going to happen next,
I scream, 'Mum, Dad are you alright?'

Charlotte Shearer (11)
Ellesmere College, Ellesmere

Christmas Time

Snow falling from the treetops
Like crispy leaves in autumn,
The snow landing softly,
White, cold and good fun!

Children playing,
Building snowmen and having snowball fights,
Not wanting to stop for tea!

Up in the hills the older kids play,
Not wanting to be noticed.
Playing with sledges,
Smiling and laughing!

Children start to disappear
Leaving carrots and cherries for Santa,
Climbing into bed excitedly.

Waking up in the morning
Jumping out of bed,
Running towards the tree,
Has Santa come?

Presents waiting
Santa's been, cherries gone
And the carrots,
Opening presents with glee!

Rosie Rickett (11)
Ellesmere College, Ellesmere

Fear Poem

It was Hallowe'en night at the end of the year,
All alone in the park with no one but my fear,
The tower struck ten as the streetlights came on,
The screech of the trick or treaters
I was the only one.
The statues on the fountains looked like ghosts,
I wish I were at home the most.
No one was there, there was no crowd
The silence was so quiet it was loud!
It was scary, it was frightening,
Luckily there was no lightning.
Although my skin has goosebumps
My hairs were standing up too.
Here's a priceless piece of advice,
Never stay out when there are no lights!

Samantha Wolfson (12)
Ellesmere College, Ellesmere

Hallowe'en Haikus

The wolves are biting,
Coming for little children,
Maybe even more.

Children are screaming
Shadows creeping through the night,
Candy is spilling.

The witches waking,
Broomsticks flying in the night,
Children in a fright.

Marcus Birkin (11)
Garibaldi College, Mansfield

September The 11th

It was on this day a disaster would happen
People running on feet to Manhattan
People cryin' that family members were dying,
For it was this day the Twin Towers were lost.

The plane was flying overhead
The plane was gleaming
People were screaming when the plane hit,
I thought I was dreaming.

I'll call 911; the fire brigade came quicker than ever
They described the towers as hanging on by a tether
The firemen went in, it started to topple
The firemen gasped, the towers collapsed!

Why did Bin Laden plot this fate?
People being dug up, it's a horrible wait
Thinking back on what had happened,
People jumping, planes exploding
This is a day we will never forget.

Jack Parnwell (13)
Garibaldi College, Mansfield

Hallowe'en Haikus

People dressing up,
Now excited and nervous
And jump out the door.

Knocking at the door,
Toy witches sensing you there,
Laughing hauntedly.

The door pings open,
Children screaming, 'Trick or treat!'
Chocolates fill their bags.

Rebecca Holloway (11)
Garibaldi College, Mansfield

The Deadly Side Of Hallowe'en!

Hallowe'en is here,
Hang a cross above your bed,
Hallowe'en is here.

The witches cackling
Wolves whistling, ghouls scaring kids,
Kids egging houses.

Spirits roam the earth,
The mean dead become undead,
Slowly bringing doom!

Hallowe'en has gone,
Take the cross down from your bed,
Hallowe'en has gone!

Victoria Gelsthorpe (11)
Garibaldi College, Mansfield

The Beach

The sunlight shines on the sand,
In colours of gold and brown,
Sand trickles through my fingers
And falls back onto the soft ground.

The waves overlap, blue and green,
The rock pools nearby
Have little fish and seaweed
Floating and swimming about.

Palm trees stretch high into the sky,
Coconuts fall from the huge leaves,
I step away and watch,
Then I walk off . . .

Sarah Chandler (13)
Garibaldi College, Mansfield

A Day In The Life Of School

School is a scary place,
When you walk in the door it
Gives you such a shiver.
Meeting teachers face to face
Is enough to make you quiver.

First you have registration
Which is not so bad.
You meet your form tutor
And find out he is really mad.

Before you know it, it is break
And your brain begins to ache
And they serve lots of different cake.

Not it's time to go upstairs for lesson three
Stopping the lift halfway
To scare your TA.

Ring, the bell goes, it's time for lunch
Off the kids go *munch, munch, munch*.
Eating, eating, looking to choose
Or ordering your meal, sandwiches,
Crisps drink that's the deal.

Now it's lesson four, nearly time to go,
Just one more hour, what a bore!
Then the bell goes and home you go.

School wasn't so bad after all.

Daniel Jones (13)
Garibaldi College, Mansfield

Nature

I cut through the sky
Prey be warned I hunt at night
Kill with beak and claws
What am I . . . ?

Thomas Helmkay (13)
Garibaldi College, Mansfield

Broken Home

I sat and watched my dad,
As he walked right out the door.
I stood and watched my family,
As it broke and tore.

I heard my mother crying
As she nursed her broken arm.
I saw my brother trying,
To keep my sister calm.

I know I won't see my dad again,
He picked the perfect time to leave.
I know this year isn't full of joy,
Because he left on Christmas Eve.

When my older brother came home,
He knew exactly what was going on.
It happens all to often,
It all started back when I was one.

Now my family is better off,
'Cause my dad isn't here.
My brothers, my sister, my mum and I,
No longer live in fear.

Tanisha Guy (14)
Garibaldi College, Mansfield

Hallowe'en Kids Haikus

Mean Hallowe'en ghosts
Haunting houses, scaring kids
Spinning round and round.

Trick or treating kids
Wearing frightening costumes
Scaring other kids.

Scary kids at night
They really are a good fright,
And they look spooky!

Grant Davidson (11)
Garibaldi College, Mansfield

Hallowe'en Haikus

Ghosts, ghouls, vampires,
They are my favourite things
As well as witches.

Carving of pumpkins
The day of All Hallows Eve
Time of dressing up.

Knocking on the doors
The time for trick or treating
And eating sweeties.

Dressed up for parties
Shopping for all the costumes
Trying them all on.

Counting all the sweets
Sorting them all into piles
Gobble them all up.

Giving out the sweets
Children are all excited
Bags stretched wide open.

Liane Powell (11)
Garibaldi College, Mansfield

Hallowe'en Haikus

It's time to dress up,
And trick or treat, *knock, knock, knock*
We are at the door.

Witches are cackling
Scary ghosts and whistling wolves at night
Children having fun.

Hallowe'en is gone
Time to stop trick or treating
Hallowe'en is gone.

Zoe Godfrey (11)
Garibaldi College, Mansfield

The Sea

The waves are rough, the current goes east
It flows past a seagull's nest,
Surfers ride the waves, while divers dive
Under the sea, what different wonders.

Crabs, squids and fish all swim around
Friends and foes, nobody knows
Watch out for the killer sharks
Jumping up and down, here's the dolphin.

The sea will live forever
The coldness kills like 15 knives
Seven seas, seven different places
What hides underneath, no one knows.

So many creatures live underneath
So many plants that live there
So many wonders that the sea holds
So many treasures hidden down there.

The sea shines in the sun
The sea glistens in the sun
The sea shows us our reflections
The sea is a wondrous place.

Natalie Swain (13)
Garibaldi College, Mansfield

Hallowe'en Haikus

I knock at the door,
And then I say 'trick or treat!'
And I get some sweets.

Everyone dressed up,
All in their scary costumes,
Having lots of fun.

People have parties
Then set off some fireworks,
They light up the sky.

Paige Matthews (11)
Garibaldi College, Mansfield

My Happy Family

My dad's in a foul mood,
I don't think I should be rude,
My brother marched out of the door,
I think my family's tore.

My mum's in tears,
Why isn't anything clear?
I feel like I started it,
I want to fall into a bottomless pit.

My dad's shouting at my mum,
Why is my family so dumb?
I think I should leave,
I don't know what to believe.

I heard the slam of a car door,
I could not believe what I saw,
My dad zoomed out the drive,
I hope my brother's still alive.

I rushed downstairs to check things out,
But I could not find my mum about,
I sat down and began to wonder,
All of a sudden it began to thunder.

I ran outside to look for my brother,
Should I go this way or the other?
I decided to go left not right,
In the dead of the night.

I ran down to the bottom lane,
Then I felt a sharp pain,
I woke up; I'm not dead,
But I was alone in a hospital bed.

Amy Gillespie (13)
Garibaldi College, Mansfield

Snowy Night

I woke up one night
Because I had a fright
I looked out the window and saw the snow,
With its white, sparkling, twinkling glow.

The brightness of the moon
Made it like it happened so soon.
With the shine of the snowflake,
When it hit the ground it looked like icing off a cake.

Everyone is wrapped in coats,
It makes us look like floats.
We had a lot of fights with snowballs,
The hiders hid behind all the halls.

I went down the snowy hill,
Next to the big, wooden mill.
When I was going home I'd seen a model head,
When I got home I went straight to bed.

I just got in my bed and lay,
I couldn't sleep because it was nearly Xmas day.
I grabbed the stuff I wanted to keep,
Just before I went to sleep.

When I woke up I was glad,
But my cousin went a bit mad!
All the presents were fun,
Then the snow melted when what appeared, the sun!

Conor Boothey
Garibaldi College, Mansfield

A Cold Winter's Day

A cold winter's day, the snow is falling
In the distance a robin is calling
Putting on my hat and gloves
I see a pair of snow-white doves.

Seeing a robin flying high
Eating a piece of apple pie
People playing in the snow
Hearing Santa, 'Ho, ho, ho!'

People having a snowball fight
Making a snowman, big and white
Children's faces are so red
I think they might be ready for bed.

The moon is shining brighter than ever
Children hope the snow lasts forever
Tucked up tight in their beds
Thoughts of Santa in their heads.

James Allsopp (13)
Garibaldi College, Mansfield

Hallowe'en Haikus

Late on a dark night
The night to give you a fright
It's not a good sight.

Witches in black hats
The dark sky all full of bats
Broomsticks and black cats.

Spooks and ghouls are seen
Trick or treaters have all been,
Happy Hallowe'en.

Kristie Wathall (11)
Garibaldi College, Mansfield

The Circus Goes Wrong

The big red tent, the big funny clowns.
That looks fun, let's go down.
There it is, I can see it from here.
I could probably see it if I was at the pier.

The clowns run around, the lions are roaring.
There are people in the sky and my dad is still snoring.
As I hear the music play,
I can see some of the animals eating their hay.

A man from the sky has fallen into a net
There's a man with a lion, and he's making it look like a pet.
Then it bit off his big fat head
And guess what? Now he is dead!

We have got away, so now we're okay
But now he is back so we've got to run away.
I am now at home in my cosy bed
So now I will live and I will not be dead.

Alexander Gibson (13)
Garibaldi College, Mansfield

Hallowe'en Haikus

Hallowe'en is here
Kids dressed as scary monsters
Hope the fun will last.

A cast of a spell
Ring a doorbell, get a treat
Perhaps give a trick.

A floating ghost *whoo* . . .
Something scary at the door
That makes you jump far.

Holly Brailsford (11)
Garibaldi College, Mansfield

White Wedding

Everyone entered the church with a smile,
Even though they had walked a mile,
They all waited for the arrival of the bride,
Finally she arrived and everyone sighed.

Grab the bouquet of flowers and walk down the aisle,
Meet the groom and give him a smile,
You will be getting married very soon,
Then you will be ready for your honeymoon.

Say all of the vows and please say, 'I do,'
Then kiss the bride and say, 'I really love you,'
Then throw your confetti all over their heads,
But still make sure that they look their best.

When they come out the snow did fall,
Their dream of a white wedding came true after all,
Then they went to the party and danced when in love,
As the snow fell down from up above.

Zoey Marples (13)
Garibaldi College, Mansfield

Hallowe'en Haikus

Apple bobbing fun,
Trick or treat, candy or sweet
Scary or hairy.

Darkness swirl, moonlight
Hubble, bubble cauldron stir
Night loom Hallows Eve.

Scary party fun
Tricks galore, excitement pours
Lots of sweets for me.

William Hall (11)
Garibaldi College, Mansfield

Hurricane Ivan

Hurricane Ivan broke out
Everyone in Jamaica was running about.
Disaster had struck
They had run out of luck.

They had nowhere to run
And the children weren't having fun.
They had nowhere to hide
As the men tried to take it in their stride

Houses had fallen down
While people were run out of town
The end was near,
They quivered with fear.

Many people had died
As the mourners stood side by side.
As tears ran down people's faces
People had vanished without a trace.

Frances Woolley (13)
Garibaldi College, Mansfield

Hallowe'en Haikus

Monsters or witches
Trick or treat, something scary
Magic or dressing up, magic!

Trick or treat, scary
Pumpkins and spiders with webs
Hallows Eve night swirls.

Lollipops or tricks
Trick or treat something scary
Magic with witches.

Abbey Haynes (11)
Garibaldi College, Mansfield

People I'll Never Meet

People I'll never meet like Britney Spears, Raven, Sean Paul,
The list goes on,
The only time I'll see a star is on the TV
And before you know it they're gone,
Concerts are OK,
But you can only see them from far away,
These people I'll never meet.

Concerts cost too much money though,
And the money in my piggy bank is very low,
To meet a star would be really ace,
To ask them what it's like to be famous
And wear fancy dresses made of lace,
These fancy people I'll never meet.

But there are only three people that I really, really want to meet,
These three boys at the 'Brit Awards' that would be hard to beat
These three lads rock so bad,
Knowing I'll never meet Busted makes me mad,
These three boys I'll never meet.

Danni Rushby (13)
Garibaldi College, Mansfield

Hallowe'en Haikus

A knock at the door
Trick or treat has come to you
And people are scared.

Scaring you like mad
Ghouls and ghosts come to get you
And people go boo!

Pumpkins are outside
Children getting lots of sweets
And adults get scared!

Dean Haywood (11)
Garibaldi College, Mansfield

The War In Iraq

Passing the bells for the people in Iraq,
The monstrous anger of guns attack, attack,
We keep fighting with the strutting rifles rattling,
And still they keep on fighting.

The hot, dry conditions, no water to drink,
There's nowhere to wash, there really is a stink,
The bombs are coming, take cover,
For the people back home could lose a lover.

Look out Tony Blair the protesters come,
It's cold in Iraq and their lips are numb,
They're fighting for their country and for peace,
And the terrorists call for the hostage's release.

Is it worth fighting with guns and knives?
We're fighting terrorism, not losing lives,
We must keep fighting, attack,
But what do *you* think about the war in Iraq?

Joe Hessey (13)
Garibaldi College, Mansfield

Summer

The sun is shining, drying up all the rain,
Slap on the sun cream, it's summer once again.
The green grass, the bright flowers,
Hot summer days with very long hours.
Grab your sunglasses, have a water fight,
The gentle breeze, just enough to fly a kite.
Birds soaring, not a cloud in the sky,
Wasps and bees, the annoying buzz of the fly.

Bring the picnic don't forget the cake,
Buy an ice cream, sprinkles and a flake.
Summer went fast, I don't want to go back to school,
Fun-packed days, playing in the pool.
It's all over, it's all in the past now,
I have got to get ready for school, goodbye, ciao!

Laura Baxter (13)
Garibaldi College, Mansfield

School Is Open

The gates are open; let's go in,
Hundreds of kids, what a din!
Walk to form, push and shove,
Oh look there it's my big bruv.

Teachers plenty, old and new,
But for lessons I only have a few.
Coffee in the staff room, biscuits at break,
Looks like the science teacher's hair needs a rake.

Kicking of pop cans, spitting of gum,
It seems the caretaker's works never done.
The bell goes for dinner; they're all in a rush,
There are plenty of chips left, you don't have to push.

The afternoon lessons are really quite boring,
I'm falling asleep; I'll soon be snoring.
The end of school, bell goes, look at them run,
Now it's my time to start to have fun.

Rachael Hammond (14)
Garibaldi College, Mansfield

My Funeral Day

I was there on my funeral day
All my troubles seemed so far away
People in black dresses singing my favourite song
My family knew I was gone for long,
The vicar said a few words for me
I wanted people to be happy with glee
But my family were not happy;
They were sad, not glad.
We stepped outside into the cold, misty air
Oh I did wish I were at the fair,
I got lowered in the ground
I did not make a sound
For people would know
I was still around . . .

Jessica Towns (13)
Garibaldi College, Mansfield

The Unsinkable Ship

The Titanic was called the unsinkable ship,
A dream come true and a fantastic trip.

A journey from Ireland to America,
A new start for Derek, Ruth and Erica.

If only they had known what was in store,
They never would have left the safety of the shore.

Happy hearts and smiling faces,
Excitement of emptying bags and cases.

A ship so proud to sail the seas,
Did they not know the sea could freeze?

An iceberg, large and full of danger,
People screaming and help from strangers.

But now Derek, Ruth and Erica,
Could not live in America.

As the front of the Titanic started to give away,
Within 15 minutes the ship would lay.

People struggled to get free,
From the freezing cold of the Atlantic Sea.

Never forget the people the Titanic has taken,
The ghosts of the sea to never be awaken.

Alix Waddell (13)
Garibaldi College, Mansfield

Football

F ootball is the best sport ever
O wen slips the ball through to Ronaldo
O ver the bar he smashes the ball
T he keeper punts it up the field again
B eckham intercepts with precise control
A trademark Beckham pass is played over the top
L uis Figo traps the ball
L ooping it in for Zidane to score!

Niall Haslam (13)
Garibaldi College, Mansfield

The Cricket Match

The clock strikes two, we will play
The umpire says it's a wonderful day
We have the first ball but it was a wide
Everyone watched as the baby cried.

The batsman starts hitting some runs
As we all gather and eat some buns
We get back to play
And the bowler keeps the batsman at bay.

The batting team are storming along
But they lose a wicket and the fielders sing a song
The other team bat, they hope to get the required rate
The fielding team start using them as bait.

It's a close match but who will win?
It really depends on who can hit the bin
The fielders dive to stop the ball
They are acting like a stone brick wall.

Callum Charity (13)
Garibaldi College, Mansfield

My White Wedding

My big day is here I just can't wait
To walk down the aisle I'm feeling great
To tell him I love him more than ever
To wear my dress that's as white as a feather
I walk down the aisle and look at the crowd
I can hear the bells ringing there loud
I get to the bottom I said I love you
He looked right back at me and said I do too
It all went quiet the crowd stopped to sigh
At the lovely white dove we had let off to fly
We said all our vows we got them all right
We thanked the vicar for being polite
We finished the wedding my husband swallowed his pride
Finally he did it; he kissed me, the bride.

Kayleigh Marshall (13)
Garibaldi College, Mansfield

A Cold Winter's Day

A cold winter's day all cold and wet.
A cold winter's day makes everyone upset.
Cuddle with a quilt and some hot cocoa or tea.
Sat all cosy in front of the TV.

All of the snows like a big dust sheet.
Put thick socks and wellies on your feet.
Playing in the snow having a snowball fight.
Making really big snowmen all tall and white.

All the white snow it's an amazing thing.
Hear the robin redbreast's lovely singing.
Winter days are nothing, compared to how long they are in summer.
Santa rolls down the street in his brand new Hummer.

In winter it's all cold, your nose and ears go red.
Put a scarf and woolly hat on your head.
Get inside and get warm in front of the fire.
You have to put chains or knobbles on your car tyre.

Corey Alvey (13)
Garibaldi College, Mansfield

Extreme Kite Sports

K ings of the game, handling the fame
I ntercepting the wind, a web of tricks has been spinned
T rue power of the gust, doing tricks is a must
E xtreme freestyle actions, points are satisfaction.

S omething attacking, something whacking
P erfect sea breeze, we have a break and eat cheese
O n the top of the wave, battling Dave
R iding a storm, the sea starts to warm
T ampering with power, riding for an hour
S lide into first, big tricks come out in a burst.

Tom Waddingham (13)
Garibaldi College, Mansfield

September 11th

September 11th was a terrible day
Lots of people's lives were thrown away
Lots of people watching the plane fly through the air
Everyone in the city stopped to stare.

As the first plane came ploughing through
It gave all the civilians a rather big boo
Everyone nearby thought that this was a disastrous day
As lots of family lives had to pay.

As all the children were having a play
Their mums and dads thought this was a horrendous day
All about there were people running around
But all you could hear was a terrible sound.

As the second plane came shuddering through
All the civilians knew that the Twin Towers were blew
Everyone's families were screaming and shouting.

Matthew Hollis (13)
Garibaldi College, Mansfield

A Poem For Pam

Where did Pam go, nobody knows?
Way up high where no one goes,
When she went to bingo, she would win lots of money,
She would come to our house and be so funny,
When we moved to Mansfield,
She brought me right on in.

Pam's hair was gold and curly,
Her nails were always painted pink or purple,
That nice blue dress she wore for an anniversary.

Even though she's gone now,
I never will forget the fun times she shared with me,
Those days felt like they would never end.

Kirsten Tackie (13)
Garibaldi College, Mansfield

The Infants

My teacher was ugly and tall
He wore pale, thin trousers and a shirt.
I remember him falling over all the time.
He made me feel bored and sometimes good.
I loved the way he changed the lessons to art.
I hated the way he always blamed me,
He was always smiling and laughing.
The walls were covered in coloured paper.
In the corner we picked the wallpaper off the wall
Where I was used to going.
The air smelt of beans in the afternoon.
All I could hear was teachers screaming down kid's ears
The playground was like a bit of a wonderland
We always used to play on the steps
And mess around with the footballs.

Sam Waterfall (13)
Highfields School, Matlock

The Infants

My teacher was a nice big person.
She wore a dress and jumper
I remember she wore glasses
She made me feel grown-up
I loved the way she taught us
I hated the way she told me off.

The walls were covered with pictures
In the corner was a computer
Where you could do work.
The air smelt like a jungle
The playground was like a busy town
We played soldiers and guns at playtime
I always played with my best friend
Tristan and me are still friends today
I really enjoyed infant school.

Connor Boyes (13)
Highfields School, Matlock

We Are Not What We Seem

The next time you pass a stranger, look into their eyes,
Tell me, are they smiling or living through a lie?

For hidden underneath a smile, a person can be screaming,
And no one knows how much it hurts, to pray that they are dreaming.

Do those lines carved through their face, show-off a life of laughter,
Or is it pain, deep within, displayed for decades after?

Some say that people's silence should be hailed as if a blessing,
But when no one dares to speak their mind, no one is confessing.

Violent waves of anger can hurtle down a spine,
And all we do is shrug and say that everything is fine.

Surprising how a person can live through such pretence,
Spend a lifetime building up a fort of self-defence.

And so we worship perfect people, whose lives we wish to borrow,
To sugar-coat our emptiness and neutralise our sorrow.

By polluting ourselves with terror, we've turned our world so cold,
Now our lives are just a waiting place, to dream and then grow old.

We all are plagued by secrets, that sicken us to the bone,
We say that we're together, but in our hearts we are alone.

Every person in this life, can drown within from sin,
And though we fight to stay afloat, we can never win.

The world outside is wrought with cruelty, that's deepening the hole,
So we keep out hearts protected, cocoon our very soul.

How sad that love can reach so deep and never is expressed,
Our hearts can ache for lifetimes and never be at rest.

So we soldier on proclaiming that 'We're living out our dreams,'
But a lesson learnt for those who trust; we are not what we seem.

Faye Kilburn (16)
Highfields School, Matlock

Diazepam

Her world full of sadness,
Her kids full of hope,
Her eyes well with tears,
Her breath speaks with smoke.

Today she'll speak,
Head filled with a mist, confusion.
Unable to see straight, with tears in her eyes.
Relentless noise, the screaming, the sobs,
From the monster upstairs.
Incident
Rush of adrenalin,
Blood pulsating,
Temper rising,
Anxiety soars.
Think, something to end the pain.
Now in the bathroom, reach for the steel,
Choking on her breath she'll glimpse the mirror
As that trusty metal finds her arms, neck and face.
Still. Red. Calm.

The constant cycle,
Patterned tiles sparkling, red, silver shapes.
Empty packets and bottles,
Mindlessly strewn on the floor.
Finally. Sweet release.

Her world full of sadness,
Her heart filled with pain,
That man from the past,
Still screams through her veins.

Ceri Thorpe (16)
Highfields School, Matlock

The Infants

My teacher was tall and slim
She wore shiny shoes and smart green boots
She made me feel cool.
I loved the way she gave us chocolate treats each Friday
It made my day.

I hated the way she dressed in her smart green boots
The walls were covered in blue palette paint
In the corner there was a computer where you could play games.
The playground was like clattering cars
We cracked jokes in the playground.

We played football
We even played spin the bottle
I loved my school, because it was Darley Dale School
It was really, really cool
We had a naughty stool
The classroom was really dull.

Thomas Crowder (12)
Highfields School, Matlock

My Teacher

My teacher was tall and thin
He wore a tie, long trousers and a shirt
I remember he liked writing stories
He made me feel like I belonged to the school.
I loved the way he put me in the football matches every time.
The walls were covered in paint
In the corner was a big cupboard
Where everyone thought he went in to smoke
The room smelt of air freshener
The playground was like a big football pitch
We played football
I liked it.

Chris Wayne (12)
Highfields School, Matlock

The Infants

My teacher was tall with blonde hair
She wore a blouse and skirt.
I remember she told me off when we were reading a book
I had to sit under her feet
She made me feel embarrassed
I loved the way she gave me a stamp on my hand when I was good.
I hated the way she didn't help me with my work.
The walls were covered in the alphabet letters and stories
In the corner is where we used to sit and read with her,
Where it was boring!
The room smelt of bleach
As the cleaner rattled with all her jewellery
The playground was like an obstacle course
We used to play 'Simon says'
As my class was in a line to get ready for dinner.
Also we used to play heads down thumbs up when it was raining.
I hated the school dinners and I hated the mush peas.
When I left that school I missed it a lot
I miss all my favourite teachers
But I loved the Christmas dinners!

Rachel Quinn (12)
Highfields School, Matlock

The Infants

My teacher was not nice
He wore a tie, shirt and trousers.
He made me feel beastly
I hated the way he shouted.
The walls were covered in paper
In the corner stood a desk
Where the teacher sat
The room smelt of deodorant
The playground was small with nothing to do.
We played football and tig
I do not miss my infant school
The teachers there were dreadful.

Dale Travis (12)
Highfields School, Matlock

Moon Cat

She prowls the moonlit streets,
Her leathery paws gently caress the pavement
As she takes her midnight stroll
Her darkened silhouette against the garden wall,
Her shadow slowly fades into nothingness
As the church clock sounds evening,
Her coat glimmers strangely as a car passes, its headlamps aglare
Each delicate strand, highlighted as it calls the moon,
Her lamp-like eyes reveal her true beauty,
Each like emeralds emerging from a majestic place,
She wanders back to where she came from,
A place unknown,
Until the time comes again
When all is still,
And the world in its deep slumber,
She will return,
She is the moon cat.

Tom Knowles (13)
Malvern College, Malvern

Sunrise

The sunlight filtered into the beach,
Turning the night to powder opaqueness,
The warmth of the rays spread as far as one can reach
The light gained intensity
The beach took on a new colour,
A spectrum of red, yellow, green, blue, gold
The golden light moved lower,
Seeping through the palm trees
The golden sand seemed to grow even more golden,
At last the golden rays flooded in,
Just like the tide of the sea,
I watched the sunrise with awe,
How beautiful could the colours be.

Leo Manibhandu (14)
Malvern College, Malvern

Dead End

Not left, not right
Not down, not forward
Only up or back.

Left, houses and gardens
Right, houses and gardens
Forward, brick cement.

Up, sky, cloud
Back road, pavement
Forward, brick cement.

Up, way out
Back, way out
Forward, brick cement.

Bob Stirling (13)
Malvern College, Malvern

Autumn

The harvest's collected
The witch's aren't out
The summer has ended
So autumn's about.

The children are mourning
Summer's sudden dead end
They're hoping and praying
That rain's not the trend.

The ninth month has ended
The tenth just begun
The wind has just lended
The leaves some cursed fun.

For when the leaves dance,
They'll fall off the trees,
Leaving nowhere to hide
From Winter's harsh breeze.

When the last leaf has fallen,
And Jack Frost is stuck fast
There's no way that men
Can haul back Autumn's mask.

Lily Sanders (13)
Malvern College, Malvern

The Night

Black as charcoal
With spots of light
Mysterious things happen
In the night

Animals are sleeping
Everything is still
The owls watch the mist
Cover the hill

The air is cold
There is not a sound
The moon is smiling sweetly
And looking at the ground

Finally it's morning
The dew is on the wall
The animals are waking up
The cockerel has sent his call

Night is not far away
With spots of light
Mysterious things could happen
Tonight.

Lucille Perry (14)
Malvern College, Malvern

Once More . . .

Great, another go on the water,
Another chance to get close to perfect.
A chance to glide along the water's surface
And to send the water pooling.

Whoosh! I feel the boat flying,
Flying gracefully on the water.
I think of arms, swing, slide and catch
Ten full strokes without falter.
Now some power!

Oh no, too much
The boat is wobbling.
The water suddenly close and threatening
Stop!

OK, all right, calm, I start again
Arms, swing, slide and catch
Eight, nine and ten again
Maybe this time I'll get it right.

Robert Killick (14)
Malvern College, Malvern

Sunlight And Snow

Smiles and tears,
Sunlight and snow:-
The world shines,
The world glows.

Spring brings the twinkling dew,
The sun shines bright the summer through,
Autumn has its glowing golds and browns
And Winter's glittering snow falls to the ground.

Let the world shine,
Let your heart glow,
Through all the sunlight
And all of the snow.

Sarah Stilliard (14)
Malvern College, Malvern

Bogey At The First

Addressing the ball at the first tee
I'm feeling nervous; it's all down to me.
I take an almighty swing
It hits a tree with a hollow ping.
A second later, I hear a plop
Oh dear, oh dear not even a free drop.

Here I stand no longer on the tee
Tragically, already taken three
Now I need a fantastic approach
Just like the one I practised with my coach
I hit it sweetly, it goes like a dream
And holds up nicely on the green.

About to play my first putting shot
I desperately want to make the pot.
I crouch right down to inspect the line
I think I've got it right, just fine.
A fifteen footer might not be that rare
But this one means I'm still all square.

William Bishop (13)
Malvern College, Malvern

Night

While daylight takes the horizon for its bed
And the stars make visible their glorious heads
The moon sits puffing on a cloudy cigar
Shining its beauty like a gem from afar
The whisper of the trees like a secret untold.
The dancing of the trees to a rhythm, but behold!
The curtains close
The lights turn off
Your eyes open for the last time then . . .

Ayobami Afolabi
Malvern College, Malvern

My Family

I have a mum and dad and sister,
I love my family.
We live in a house full of noise because:
We work together
And laugh together,
We live together
And love together
We do things together,
The shopping,
The gardening,
The cooking,
And I like cleaning the house.
We work together as a team,
Working, helping, doing, loving,
And I love my family.

Brian Hanslow (16)
Quince Tree School, Tamworth

Hurt Feelings

Some people hurt my feelings.
They do it either to wind me up or to try to upset me
People say things to me like 'Shut up'
Or the say words I don't like 'Don't'
They are unappreciative of how I do things
If I'm told how I could have done things differently
That pretty much hurts my feelings.

Inside I get upset
And outside the tears slide down my face
I feel hot on the outside
And my throat dries up.

Why don't you try to understand me?
And where I'm coming from
And don't hurt my feelings?

Adam Burd (16)
Quince Tree School, Tamworth

At The Airport

I see aeroplanes taking off - going somewhere nice.
People are getting on planes,
Others standing at the desks,
Asking for the right plane, for the right flight.
Time to go to departure
Waiting, waiting, waiting and waiting for . . .
'The plane is ready . . .'
People go to the right plane
They go on the plane
They sit on their seats
The doors are closed . . .
And the plane goes to the main runway, wait
Until . . . they clear for take-off
They they're off . . . bumpy as they go up, up and
Up, off somewhere nice, through the sky.

And I am at the airport,
Watching . . .
Not going anywhere . . .
Except in my dreams.

Brett Jennings (16)
Quince Tree School, Tamworth

My Uncle Mark

My uncle Mark is tall,
He wears glasses,
He has short hair,
He looks after me.
But best of all,
He brings stuff home.
He gets games from his mates for me,
PlayStation 2 games.
Then he watches as I kill people, kill cops
And get the high score!
He's my mate.

Stephen Baker (16)
Quince Tree School, Tamworth

Spain

The sun is hot.
I get burnt,
Burnt a lot.

The noise is girls screaming,
Screaming at the pool,
Screaming to their friends.

I go round visiting people -
Friends from England
Friends who live in Spain.

I'm going out tonight,
Out for a meal,
Chips just like in England.

Get a beer,
Got to go shopping with Mum,
It's good.

After four days
I want to go home,
I think I am going back next Saturday.

Craig Berrow (18)
Quince Tree School, Tamworth

Heartache

My head hurts when I can't see my friends anymore
My heart aches, a dull feeling all the time
But when I think of them my heartache is sharp.

My head hurts when I think my boyfriend's cheating on me
It cuts like a knife - a stab through my heart.

My head hurt when my grandfather died
It is sore when I think about him.
My mum is hurting - her head is also hurting inside.

Georgina Unwin (17)
Quince Tree School, Tamworth

My Dog Ben

He's as black as night
He's as bright as a science teacher
He's as quiet as a mouse
But he's poorly because he's as blind as a bat.

He licks people
He climbs on the settees
He likes going in cars
He likes eating
He's friendly
He wags his tail
He runs a lot.

He comes up to me and nuzzles me
He licks my hand
We go for walks together
I talk to him
I love him.
He's my best friend.

Lee Goodfellow (16)
Quince Tree School, Tamworth

On Holiday

I go to Skegness with my family
And we stay in a big caravan.
There's a lot to do on the holiday
Imagine it - see if you can.

I get to ride at the fairground
The teacups turn me around
I can make sandcastles
By piling the sand in a mound.

See all the fish, see the boats
In the sea, on the sea,
Play in the water, splash, and paddle
And swim in the sea.

Donna Allen (17)
Quince Tree School, Tamworth

Jessica

She was my best friend
We played together
Made a mess -
Made mum mad.

Round and round we ran together
Until we were out of breath
Flopped down on the ground . . .
Collapsed!

She ate and drank and I watched.
Wrinkled her nose
Twitching her nose
With pleasure.

Now she's gone
And I am lonely
Missing Jessica,
My beautiful rabbit.

Samantha McIntyre (16)
Quince Tree School, Tamworth

Broken Treaty

The agreement has been shattered
The pact is dead
The alliance has been corrupted
Prepare for blood to shed.

The bargain has been sabotaged
The arrangement is deceased
The contract has been decimated
The death toll will increase.

The settlement has been extinguished
The civilians begin to cry
The treaty has been obliterated
It seems the end is nigh.

Tom Newby (13)
Retford Oaks High School, Retford

The Chair, The Cat And The Little Girl

Shedding tears down her large, peachy face
Lonely as if she was a lost suitcase,
Longing for just one friend
Was this it for the end?

Feeling so gloomy and glum
One day her true friend would come,
Sat there crying, wearing away
Hoping someone would come and play.

The little girl sat on her chair
She was alone but nobody gave a care,
Dark and dismal she'd find her partner soon
Staring and gazing into the bright moon.

Wishing someone was there every hour
Shut away in a shadowed tower,
She heard a cat with a delightful purr
So now there's the chair, the cat and her.

Emma Woollard (13)
Retford Oaks High School, Retford

The War

It was sweltering hot
And the war was at its worst
People were crying
While bombs flew out of the sky and burst.

Guns were firing
While bombs were flying
'Stop!' shouted the people
'They are all dying.'

Crash, boom, bang!
Stop, stop, stop!

There are no winners in war - not one!
So just *stop*.

Ellie Whitmore (13)
Retford Oaks High School, Retford

To My Grandad Bill

Every time I think of you,
The world just disappears,
And all I know is you are here,
When I'm down in tears.

I think about you all the time,
Now you are not around,
It makes me upset every day,
I'm normally in a frown.

Sometimes I hold my feelings in,
And I try to be strong,
But after a bit it gets too much,
And I just let them run.

But I don't care what people think,
'Cos it's my life not theirs,
Some people are OK about it,
And some don't really care.

I visit your grave whenever I can,
But I feel it's not enough,
There is one thing I cannot hide,
And, Grandad, that's my love.

I feel like I am someone else,
Now you are not around,
I have changed so much right now,
Since you've been underground.

You might have gone away from me,
And we might be far apart,
But, Grandad, I want you to know,
I'll keep you in my heart.

Kelli Beech (13)
Retford Oaks High School, Retford

Saying Goodbye

A life so dearly missed
Has gone away for a while
To a war
Which I will miss
A son I know
Which will hopefully
Survive the war bliss.

My son
With a gun
Will fight for our country.

I feel a tear come from my eye
As I think of him
In the sky
In which he will fly.

To say goodbye
To my only son
My face is swept by tears.

In a few days' time
I'll write a letter
Hopefully he'll reply.

When the war ends
If he comes home
I'll make sure he never leaves me.

Charlotte Kelly (13)
Retford Oaks High School, Retford

War's Arrival

A gunshot
People fleeing fast
Panic spreading faster still
What is happening?
War is here . . .

Bang, crash, boom
Is the sound of war
Babies crying in the streets
Men running to help . . .
Bang, crash, boom.

War is here . . .
But what can we do?
Our safety is in danger
We must flee for help
Help, please, help!

Terrified
Blood running cold
Thoughts of the worst flying around
Like a spitfire
Misery.

Charlotte Kent (13)
Retford Oaks High School, Retford

Bombs And Bullets

Refugees running from the war,
That's brought violence to their door,
Mothers sob and children cry,
Fathers duck as bullets fly.

Bombs exploding all the time,
Soldiers waiting for a sign
Then they charge, one by one,
Till their bloody work is done.

Katie Meads (13)
Retford Oaks High School, Retford

Apocalypse

Stutter of the gun,
Flicker of the candle,
The emotion-cluttered face
With the pain he can handle.
Wave and wave of soldiers,
Running through the mud,
Overlapping and scarred
With innocent, human blood.
Devastated lives,
With the splinter of regret,
Death by the thousands
Caught in the Devil's net.
The world sawn in half,
Opposing dark and light,
Coming together as one
In a tsunami of death and spite.

Kyle Chapman (13)
Retford Oaks High School, Retford

Blue Whale

Blue whale swimming, swishing, splashing
Through the deep blue sea
Blue whale swimming, swishing, splashing
Opening his big, wide mouth.

Bethany White (11)
Retford Oaks High School, Retford

Crocodile!

Crocodile slithering slowly
Up the murky river
Crocodile slithering slowly
In the deep, deep water.

Joe McFarlane (11)
Retford Oaks High School, Retford

What Was The Point Of The First World War?

Eventually death came into the war,
Rich people died,
But so did the poor,
Injuries and death both felt sore,
What was the point
Of the First World War?

Millions died,
Over 20 in all,
Every day you could see,
Innocent people fall.
What was the point
What was the point
What was the point
Of the First World War?

Stuart Payling (13)
Retford Oaks High School, Retford

Why?

This war is so cruel,
It seems so unjust,
People being killed,
And lives being destroyed.
We men go away,
Defending as one,
Conditions are harsh,
And life seems unfair.
We're fighting for freedom,
Justice and harmony,
Our homes seem so far away,
We long to be there.
It's world peace that we're fighting for,
So please, Lord, bring it soon.

Elanor Kerr (14)
Retford Oaks High School, Retford

Terrorism

Why does the sun shine?
Why do poems rhyme?
Why does the cookie crumble?
Why do toddlers tumble?
Why is the grass green?
Why is meat lean?
Why does a chalkboard need chalk?
Why do eagles fly not walk?
Why does a tree have a leaf?
Why do widows suffer grief?
Why is pink for a girl?
Why do ballerinas twirl?
Why is blue for a boy?
Why is a football a toy?
Why is the moon for night?
Why does the sun shine bright?
    But one thing we do know
        Terrorism's law.

Sarah Hargreaves (14)
Retford Oaks High School, Retford

Autumn!

Autumn is here,
Leaves are turning golden brown, yellow and crimson,
They crunch under your feet as you walk along the path,
People wrapped up with woolly hats and scarves,
Trying to stay warm.

The leaves looking lifeless lying on the floor,
In despair, with no one to care,
The nights are getting longer and the days are getting shorter,
Winter is now here,
Autumn is over.

Donna Tong (14)
Retford Oaks High School, Retford

Miscarriage

The pale hand slipped from,
The love that had held no promise,
And should that sweet, red bond,
Be shattered by an anger,
An anger which burnt the waters,
Killed every living joy cell nearby,
Should it near the love and build its wall,
Or is it only the cold, black ribbon of death that could break,
The sweet, red bond,
The sweet, red bond it held so close,
No,
No, anger did not take the joy cell of the sweet, red bond,
Yes,
Yes, the cold, black ribbon of death swiped the love,
At least it had hoped it would,
Even though her sweet baby could not be heard,
Nor seen by anyone else,
Their love drove her insane,
She could not stare at the stars,
Without the sweet, red bond blocking the key to freedom,
She loved her baby that could not be seen,
Or heard by anyone else,
That's all that matters now,
That's all I needed,
That's all I wanted,
Forever,
But it wasn't what she got,
Nor did I,
My life was stolen to the sky,
Hers was chained to the earth,
Only the wall of anger parted us,
Anger had built its wall.

Amber Severn (12)
Sutton Centre Community College, Sutton-in-Ashfield

Curses

When James woke up he was a girl
He had really brilliant curls
He was wearing a dress
He wasn't impressed
When he woke up in the morning.

He went to the loo and had to sit down
He looked in the mirror with a big frown
His mum didn't notice when he walked in
She looked at him with a big grin
When he woke up in the morning.

He caught the bus
He looked nonplussed
Then he saw his mate
And started to hate
When he woke up in the morning.

He paid his fare
This was a nightmare
Let him wake up
Let no one look
When he woke up in the morning.

It couldn't be true
He felt like poo
He wanted his mum
He had pain in his tum
When he woke up in the morning.

Then he went to sleep
He was in too deep
He wanted his bed
But got hit on the head
When he woke up in the morning.

Rachel Scholes (12)
Sutton Centre Community College, Sutton-in-Ashfield

When I See You

When I see you I get so excited
You make me smile
When I see you I don't know what to do, my heart is lighted
I think about you all the while.

Words cannot describe you
I love you more than words can say
You are so pure and true
I think about you every day.

How is it possible for me to love you so much?
I dream about you every night
I feel warm inside when I feel your touch
When I think about you I hug my pillow really tight.

I love you more than words can say
And I'll never stop loving you, not even for a day.

Jessica Beardall (12)
Sutton Centre Community College, Sutton-in-Ashfield

Curses

Vicious words cast across the cold air,
To condemn another to a damned eternity,
Words of evil, bound together,
Revenge, hatred, jealousy, greed.

Spineless voices in the chilled earth,
Chanting together, plotting together,
Ready to unleash evil into the world,
Cursing for revenge, hatred, jealousy, greed.

Condemning curses, the tool of evil,
Terrible words, swirled together,
Cast to damn the lost, the confused,
For revenge, hatred, jealousy, greed.

Richard Clayton (12)
Sutton Centre Community College, Sutton-in-Ashfield

You Stole

You stole my heart, you stole my mind,
You stole the love I couldn't find.
You stole my life, heart and soul,
You stole it all, all in whole.
You stole my happiness and left the sadness,
You stole it all and left the badness.

You stole everything, it's all disappeared,
You stole my friend and now nothing is cleared.
You stole my family and ruined my life,
You stole my mind as I picked up a knife.
You stole my house and my smile,
You stole my car and drove a mile.

You stole my wishes and my fairy,
You stole my magic and gave it to Mary.
You stole my kindness and my friendship,
You stole my sweetness and brought my deepness.
You stole my heart, you stole my mind,
You stole the love I couldn't find.

Amy Taylor (12)
Sutton Centre Community College, Sutton-in-Ashfield

Beach

Down on the shore,
Where the sand tickles in your toes,
Where the sea is cold and alive,
Seagulls fly and swoop,
The waves high as a mountain,
And as cold as the South Pole.

The sea an ice cube,
The air a bag of salt,
The weather a burning fire,
The smell a swimming pool of sweat,
The people full of happiness and joy.

Melanie Cudworth (11)
Sutton Centre Community College, Sutton-in-Ashfield

My Grandad!

My grandad is really funny
And he is really kind.
I've always sat on his tummy
He's always on my mind.

He likes to go to Spain
Where it's bright
To avoid the rain
And he always loves a whisky at night.

He loves my nanny
She is really funny too
Although she can be manny
Her name is Sue.

He's never sad
That's just my grandad!

Heidi Fellows (12)
Sutton Centre Community College, Sutton-in-Ashfield

The Dark Forest!

The sky was dark,
The stars were bright,
The moon shone over the trees.

The owl stood on the branches,
Hooting very loud,
As the spiders scuttled along.

The wind whistled through the trees,
They shook and shook, the leaves blew off,
As the wolves howled with fright.

The foxes hunted for food,
As one lay dead on the ground,
And the rabbits ran past them quickly.

Hayley Buck (11)
Sutton Centre Community College, Sutton-in-Ashfield

Teachers

How come teachers shout so loud
But the children sit there smiling proud?
They nag and nag and nag some more,
Sometimes in English it's a bore!
They smack their ruler, 'Listen now!
You'll never get it and you'll be wondering how!
So sit down and don't be silly
Or you'll be at the back, on your billy!'
How come teachers sound like witches?
Moaning and groaning they give you the itches!
Wagging a finger, stamping feet!
When I go to maths it's not a treat!
'Quiet now! Quiet I say!
At lunch this is where you'll stay!
Stop it, quiet, silence around!
Right, no more lunch, no talking, no sound!'

Francesca Brooks (12)
Sutton Centre Community College, Sutton-in-Ashfield

Rabbit

Sweet like chocolate,
Quiet as a mouse,
Scampers and bounces,
In his little house.

He loves to eat carrots,
He's eaten 20 in the past,
He cannot wait for feeding time,
He runs so fast.

He's brown like caramel,
He's got pink ears like candy,
He loves to play around in his hutch,
And get all sandy.

Sharni Cross (11)
Sutton Centre Community College, Sutton-in-Ashfield

The Irish Luck
(Dedicated to my Irish grandad)

Bunches of clovers swaying away
Amongst the Irish moors
Pick one with all your luck
And walk through a heavenly door.

Full of greenery and rainbow skies
As I walk through Killarney's trees
I pick a petal from the floor
As I fall upon my knees.

I look to my left, it's something shiny
Full of sparkle and love
I crawl upon my sorrowful knees
As I'm greeted by a beautiful, white dove.

It takes me to the shining light
And I see a golden pot
I'm astonished, amazed at what I have seen
Wondering if I'm losing the plot.

I look inside and there I see
A wonderful mountain of gold
I scoop it up because it's Irish luck
And skip so merrily,

And from this day, how I say
Irish luck is grand
To have it with you every day
From the clovers of Ireland.

Catherine Geraghty (12)
Sutton Centre Community College, Sutton-in-Ashfield

Darkness

Darkness
Surrounds us all
Snatches at our bodies
It scrapes and claws and grabs at us.
It knows no limits
It blinds us to everyday objects
Confuses and loses our minds
Darkness
Darkness
God help us or
Forever we fall
Our bodies lie for the rats to eat
Our guns
By our sides
Take aim, hold steady, *fire!*
They fell to the ground like flies
Darkness
Darkness
We live
Though many did not
To go back home
See our families and friends
Their hope
Freedom, liberty
And lives rested on our shoulders
I hope we did them proud.

Melissa Burton (13)
Sutton Centre Community College, Sutton-in-Ashfield

Heartbreaker

Ever since they started back at school
Things haven't been the same
No attention for his lover
It's driving her insane.

When she looks at him and smiles
He looks straight at the floor
It's like she's gone out of his life
Her heart crumbled just like rice.

Every time she talks to him
He looks away and sighs
It's like he's a different lad but in disguise.

She goes to hug him
He moves away
She starts a conversation
He doesn't stay.

Things haven't been the same
They've finished now
The reason was another girl
He chucked away their lucky pearl.

I saw them together holding hands
As they walked down the beachy sands
Her love has gone
Now she's hunting for another one.

Josie Raffan (12)
Sutton Centre Community College, Sutton-in-Ashfield

Love!

Ever since he moved out of town,
She has been so confused and down,
Thinking of why he's gone,
All she's got left is none.

Her heart is waiting for him,
She tries to hide the love that's inside,
So cold, so dim,
Her love is wearing thin.

She really could do with him,
The lad is such a sin,
She needs him back for a fact,
She misses him more and more every day.

Ever since he moved out of town,
She has been so confused and down,
Thinking of why he's gone,
All she's got left is none.

She's lost in life,
Nowhere to run,
Her love has gone,
Forever there will be none.

Kirsty Parnill (12)
Sutton Centre Community College, Sutton-in-Ashfield

When I Get Home From School

When I get home from school,
Which I think is quite cool,
I like to play with my friends,
Until the day almost ends.

When I get home from school,
Which I think is quite cool,
I sit down and eat my tea,
Whilst watching the TV.

When I get home from school,
Which I think is quite cool,
I go outside and ride my bike,
Which I really, really like.

When I get home from school,
Which I think is quite cool,
I go on the computer and talk,
Or just simply go for a walk.

Rachel Fox (11)
Sutton Centre Community College, Sutton-in-Ashfield

My Cat

I have a cat, his name is TC,
He's loved a lot by my family and me.
He's ginger and white and he goes out at night,
He gives me a fright 'cos he's always looking for a fight.

He has big eyes that are green,
Like the greenest apples you have seen.
Like stars in the sky they shine at night,
They're so bright you don't need a light.

My TC is very nice,
But he's not as friendly with the mice.
Although he sleeps most of the day,
He comes to me when he wants to play.

Natalie Maskell (11)
Sutton Centre Community College, Sutton-in-Ashfield

The Darkness

The ceiling seems to stare at me,
As I lay in my pine bed.
Shadows cast on the walls,
As light spills through the curtain.
A buzzing noise slithers through the night air.
As the atmosphere gets colder,
Everything seems dull around me,
The doors start to creek,
And everything seems loud.
Bloodcurdling screams leak through the shadows,
Making my heart race with fear,
The underworld begins to lurk in the darkness.
My bed starts to fall,
As the darkness engulfs my mind.
The room disappears and he stands over.
His teeth start to lash, glowing in the dark,
Moving towards my neck.
Suddenly a stream of light broke through,
His face thrashed in agony.
The darkness collapsed around me,
As the light became bright.
Happiness shone through the sunlight.

Joshuah Alik Goncearenko (11)
Sutton Centre Community College, Sutton-in-Ashfield

The Farm And Market

The farm smells bad,
The spices in the market taste good,
The cows' moos are weird,
The pigs' oinks are boring,
The chickens' clucks just repeat,
There's a bald-headed farmer to meet,
The animals feel smooth to touch,
The market food feels rough.

Kimberly Barsby (11)
Sutton Centre Community College, Sutton-in-Ashfield

Me And You

If I were a dog and you were a dog,
This is what we'd do
We'd fetch our sticks and exchange lovely licks,
That is what we'd do.

If I were a cat and you were a cat,
This is what we'd do
We'd file our nails and chase mice tails,
That is what we'd do.

If I were an owl and you were an owl,
This is what we'd do
We'd eat all the rats and scare all the cats,
That is what we'd do.

If I were a snake and you were a snake,
This is what we'd do
We'd slither and slide and then we'd hide,
That is what we'd do.

If I were a shark and you were a shark,
This is what we'd do
We'd swim in slow motion in the blue ocean,
That is what we'd do.

So let's be a shark,
Not a cat, not a owl,
You choose what we shall do.

Elizabeth Whiley (12)
Sutton Centre Community College, Sutton-in-Ashfield

The Show!

Dance, prance
Whirl and twirl
Sliding, gliding
Like a swan.

Point, point, point bend
Tap, tap, tap toe
Follow the rhythm
And away we go.

Fast, slow
Hear the tempo
Soft, quiet
High and low.

I need to practise
I can't go wrong
The show is close by
2 weeks, maybe 1.

The night of the show
Finally came
No need to whistle
It's only a game.

Phew, the show has ended
I didn't step a foot wrong
I wish it had only just started
Because I had so much fun!

Laura Whittingham (12)
Sutton Centre Community College, Sutton-in-Ashfield

My Sharp Pains

Recently I found out some horrific news.
Once again the sharp pains returned.
I'm going to miss so much this summer.
Once again the sharp pains returned.
I know I shouldn't have been so selfish.
Once again the sharp pains returned.
Falling into this deep depression darkened with death.
Once again the sharp pains returned.
Worried about what life brings around the next turn.
Once again the sharp pains returned.
Not knowing what lies ahead.
Once again the sharp pains returned.
No more pain now.
The pain is gone.
So am I.

Daniel Warren (13)
Sutton Centre Community College, Sutton-in-Ashfield

Thank You

My teacher said just yesterday,
'A thank you is polite to say.
If you're polite and always kind
Others will say thanks, you'll find.'
So . . .
I shared my cold with Mike McGee,
He never gave a thanks to me.
I shared my tissue with Jo Lee,
She never gave a thanks to me.
I shared my gum with David D,
He never gave a thanks to me.
Although I rarely get it right,
I always *try* to be polite.

Natasha Donbayand (11)
Sutton Centre Community College, Sutton-in-Ashfield

Curse

Cursed for eternity, never dies,
Hell has broken loose on him,
Evil deeds happen back,
To the one who sent them out,
Every day he lies in wait,
For the person he longed to hate,
Rotting away in his cage,
Maggots crawled in his fingers,
Where his nails should be,
Holes where flesh should be,
But when the moon shows,
You'll hear him moan,
His face was never shown,
Until his sentence was death,
The noose went round his neck,
And it fell,
And broke his neck.

Mark Sanders (12)
Sutton Centre Community College, Sutton-in-Ashfield

Show Jumping

Show jumping
The horses jumping very high
They're jumping so high they touch the sky.
The fences are made from wood.
The shows are really good.
I love to watch the horses jumping.
It makes me sad to see them fall.
The sound of the horses is a clump
When they hurdle over the wall.
Show jumping is my favourite sport.
I like to see bending legs.

Jade Hagan (11)
Sutton Centre Community College, Sutton-in-Ashfield

Vamps!

Enter the world of vampires!
White faces bringing you to a halt.
Smirking and liars,
Sending you a massive bolt!
Everything you say they hear,
The things you do they see,
The movement they see.
Black capes, black drapes,
Fangs deep down into the supple skin of a screaming human!
Vampiresses sharing their evil way of love!
Killing with the soothingness of the dove.
She who takes you down with a soothing jolt!
They like to play two of a kind, eyes fulfilled with dark evilness!
The underworld of evilness with the underworld of kindness.
A whirling, dark, medieval town packed with human slayers.
Fear us, that we are vampires,
Take us down then we take you down!
With so many evil tricks but do you know them? No!
Bite to the bone when you're alone.
So now the body is alone with a stake in one hand
And two holes in the other!
Discrimination!

Coral Depledge (13)
Sutton Centre Community College, Sutton-in-Ashfield

Friends

I love you because you are my friend,
I want to stay with you until the end,
You mean the world so stay and be,
My best friend for eternity.
The way you smile and make me laugh,
I'm just so happy that you are so glad.
The good times are in our minds,
The bad times are in the past,
So please stay so we laugh and have a blast.

Nicola Shaw (11)
Sutton Centre Community College, Sutton-in-Ashfield

Curses And Superstitions

My curse is worse
It'll make you burst
There'll be no need to see the nurse
You won't be hubbly-bubbly
No more sweet and cuddly.

My curse is worse
You'll die of thirst
It's too late for the doctor or the nurse.

Don't mistake moles for holes
Or lizards for yellow-spotted wizards.

It's the worst burst
For this sort of
Curse!

Emma Wass (12)
Sutton Centre Community College, Sutton-in-Ashfield

Luke, Don't Ignore Me

This boy has been ignoring me,
And I think it's time for him to see,
It's very, very wrong.
So now he won't speak all day long,
He shall have a nasty surprise,
This shall happen at the sunrise.

The moment he wakes up,
His mouth will be covered by a cup,
He will try to get attention,
But he cannot,
So he gets out his pension
And he was left to rot.

John Wadley (12)
Sutton Centre Community College, Sutton-in-Ashfield

I Like To Wind Adam Up

I like to wind Adam up,
So he screams and shouts.
I also enjoy riding my bike,
But when I was 1 I had a trike.
I do not like carrots, cauliflower or broccoli,
My mum doesn't make me eat as much, now that's lucky.
I absolutely hate cleaning my room,
I decide to play on the PS2.
But there's one problem, I need the loo,
Then Mum shouts, 'Tea's ready.'
So I walk down the stairs very steady,
And when I get to the table it's broccoli and jelly.
So I just think,
I'd rather eat a welly!

Marc Baumanis (12)
Sutton Centre Community College, Sutton-in-Ashfield

Sadness

Sadness feels like a hole in the head,
When someone breaks your heart in two,
All you want to do is cry,
Just hoping that it's all one big, fat lie,
Eating comfort food will help you through,
Watching a good movie can help you too,
A box of tissues is something you'll need,
Forget about them, loving them was definitely a bad deed,
You'll be too upset to go and enjoy yourself,
Just hoping that they were the size of an elf.

Michael Smith (12)
Sutton Centre Community College, Sutton-in-Ashfield

Love!

Love means peace up in the air
The big, sparkly blue eyes started to stare
The passion is wonderful
They are inseparable
Everyone stares at the couple to be
Are you sure he is staring at me?
The couple are gazing, the pulses are racing
He got on one knee, filled me with glee
Shall I say yes? Shall I say no?

My heart is saying let's go.
I thought, *Will I be happy? Will I be sad?*
Will I be calm? Will I be mad?
Will I be happy in my heart?
I can't really imagine us being apart.

But you started to lie
I started to hurt
You started to sigh
I started to cry.

I said I gave up everything I had
On something that just wouldn't last
So I refused to try
I just walked and said *goodbye!*

Meg Whawell (12)
Sutton Centre Community College, Sutton-in-Ashfield

The Twin Towers

There were two towers in New York
Both looked the same,
Both tall and big,
Where can we place the blame?

Some aeroplanes crashed
Into the big white ones,
They fell down,
It was a terrifying sight.

They crashed down with a bang
And were never
To be seen
Again.

Many people died
And were injured
Because of those aeroplanes
The Twin Towers were gone.

It makes you feel angry and sad
Because those aeroplanes crashed
Into those precious Twin Towers
New York will never be the same.

Paige Whitehead (13)
The Holgate Comprehensive School, Hucknall

Hitman

I'm a storm, I'm a twister, and I'm a terrible blizzard
I'm a riddler, I'm a flyer, and I'm an evil wizard.

I'm a slayer, I'm a killer, and I'm a stylish winner,
I'm a conner, I'm a dealer, and I've a horrible inner.

I'm an athlete, I'm a runner, and I'm a one man team
I'm a dodger, I'm a gymnast, and I am really mean.

I'm exciting, I'm fantastic, and I'm a really big sport,
I'm bloodsucking, self-centred, and my hit list is short.

Phil Dearden (12)
The Holgate Comprehensive School, Hucknall

My Rose!

Shall I compare you to the moon and stars?
With a twinkling light shining against a cold, dark night
Thou heart is a single rose from a crystal vase
Your warm complexion is a delightful sight
My love for thee is strong and bold
Your voice sings lightly on the summer breeze
I love thee more than words can hold
Your eyes of gold does me please
I have always loved you but from afar
Your scent surrounds me and makes me dizzy
Your kisses are like honey from a jar
I would like to tell you but you are always far too busy
What I am trying to tell you is sonnet prose
Is that I want you to love me and be my *rose!*

Grace Carpenter (13)
The Holgate Comprehensive School, Hucknall

Suffering

Look at the world,
What do you see?
Look at the news,
How can that be?

It makes me feel sick,
It makes me feel sad.
How did the Earth,
Become so bad.

I feel guilty,
Is it my fault?
I wish it could stop,
Come to a halt . . .

Emma Mooken (12)
The Holgate Comprehensive School, Hucknall

Goose Fair

People, people everywhere,
Crowding towards the Goose Fair,
The stalls, rides and coconut shyes,
If you want fun then open your eyes,
Yellow, orange, purple, blue,
I'm having fun and so will you.

Fun, funky food and mushy peas,
The food's so cool you'll be on your knees,
Hook a duck or shooting a dart,
What will you win? Maybe a kart!
Long ago you could buy a goose,
But right back then it could run on the loose.

The rifle range, the palm reader's booth,
Going on the waltzer, that's not so smooth,
Toys, goldfish and candyfloss,
Dad's wallet is running at a loss,
Whirling, looping, going so fast,
The Goose Fair is definitely a blast!

Charlie Pates (11)
The Holgate Comprehensive School, Hucknall

The Song Of Me

I'm an angel, I'm a devil
And I need a decent level.

I'm an itch; I'm a twitch,
In the morning I'm a witch.

I'm vodka, I'm wine,
Mess with me; I'll break your spine!

I'm a plug, I'm a socket
And I hate Polly Pocket!

For I can love and I can scare,
Mess with me if you dare!

Amber Curtis (12)
The Holgate Comprehensive School, Hucknall

Goose Fair

People, people everywhere
Crowding towards the Goose Fair
Smell that smell of fantastic food
Everybody in a good mood,
Hear the sound of people screaming
All these rides flashing and gleaming.

Dodgems dodging everywhere
Feel the wind in your hair,
From the waltzers and big wheel
To candyfloss and a decent meal.
Goose Fair is the best time of year
That big roller coaster striking fear.

All the rides gleam and glide
Then someone shouts, 'Last ride!'
'Ladies and gentlemen don't lose your hair
But it's the end of the Goose Fair,'
People laugh and people cheer
Because it will be back next year.

Brenn Burbanks (11)
The Holgate Comprehensive School, Hucknall

Destruction

D estroy everything and everyone in its path
E liminating its enemies
S aving its friends
T rying to miss nothing
R eeling in death.
U nder attack, but from what?
C reating chaos
T rying to fight it
I t is a robot race
O n, off, we found the switch
N ow the weakness of an army.

Anthony Burnell (11)
The Holgate Comprehensive School, Hucknall

The Ballad Of September 11th

The people of New York
Living their everyday lives
Men of the city
Even their wives.

The people were shouting
They heard a thump
Their hearts sank
Bump! Bump! Bump!

The people screamed
The people shouted
'Oh my God!'
As the shattered glass gleamed.

What happened?
The fallen rubble
Killed so many
The terrorists are in trouble.

Go to work
Biggest of them all
Who would have thought?
It would fall.

Callum Urquhart (13)
The Holgate Comprehensive School, Hucknall

I Can't Sleep

People snoring, children whinging, doors slamming
Music playing, *I can't sleep.*
Corridor creaking, cradle rattling,
People singing, *I can't sleep.*
Taps dripping, light gleaming, people moaning
Men drinking, *I can't sleep!*

Victoria Bamford (11)
The Holgate Comprehensive School, Hucknall

Iraq

Tony, Tony, Tony,
All the lies you told,
What was the war about?
Was it about the black gold?

The soldiers went to Iraq to fight,
To help they risked their lives,
They fought and fought, many got killed,
And some lucky soldiers survived.

Sand dunes filled the landscape,
Guns and bombs attack,
Innocent men women and children,
These are victims of Iraq.

Three men were beheaded,
And some are still inside,
One was Kenneth Bigley,
The others I can't describe.

When will this war end?
What will Bush decide?
He must act quickly,
He can't just run and hide.

Louise Colton (13)
The Holgate Comprehensive School, Hucknall

The Fair!

Shouting at the children
Screaming of the adults
Crying of the babies
Singing of the roundabout
Howling of the ghost ride
And all the music beating
Fair.

Emma Maddox (11)
The Holgate Comprehensive School, Hucknall

The Ballad Of Superman

He starred in three movies
And he was Superman
He played an important part
But his life went down the pan.

He was paralysed
He fell off a horse
It must have hurt
He was a good man of course.

He needed a medic
He tried to raise money
For the paraplegic
But I bet he liked honey.

He died of heart failure
He ended up in a wheelchair
It was very sad
It should have been a premiere.

It was sad to say goodbye
He'd been through so much
Now he has gone up high
We'll all be sad without him.

Reece Foster (12)
The Holgate Comprehensive School, Hucknall

The Library

The library,
Clicking of the keyboards,
Flicking of the books,
Opening and closing of the door,
The creaking of the floor,
The squeaking of the chairs,
The sound of people moving everywhere,
The library.

Aimee Hadman (11)
The Holgate Comprehensive School, Hucknall

You Annoy Me In So Many Ways

How do you annoy me? Let me count the ways
You take the mickey out of my mother
You did this on my 14th birthday in May
You like to bully my younger brother
I wish I could hit you but it's a crime
You even dared to come round to my warm house,
If I do hit you I will get some time
You just keep on coming like a little mouse.
How do you annoy me? Let me count the ways.
You think you know everything there is to know.
Now listen this is going to stop these days
So I went up to him and said, 'No, no.'
It has now stopped let's go and play
Now my so-called friend has started today.

Niall Christie (13)
The Holgate Comprehensive School, Hucknall

Witch's Spell

Frogs' legs, rats' tails
Cats' eyes and hairy snails

Heart of goat
Man with coat

Spiders' legs,
Covered in sweaty pegs

Bird's eye
Human stomach pie

Venom of poisonous snake
With a granny's liver cake

Pig's tongue
With a smell so strong.

Macha Haskey (13)
The Holgate Comprehensive School, Hucknall

Julie Howard's Spell

For a potion that is so cruel throw in a dead frog skin
With the mouldy cheese and the wriggling maggots,
Cow's intestines full of worms
Mouldy horse brain and rotten apple
Crusty toenails throw in with a nasty cackle!

Double, double, toil and trouble, fire burn and cauldron bubble.
For the next part we will need lots of gross bits and parts
Eye of cow, brain of a frog, guts from a pig and the tongue of a dog,
Pour in a pint of ancient crusty vomit.

Everything in this spell will make you squirm.

Snake's fork, and blind worm sting,
Lizard's foot and howlet's wing
Drink, now you are a frog.

Liam Hunter (13)
The Holgate Comprehensive School, Hucknall

Witch's Spell

Tail of rat, toe of frog, rotted toenails, hair of dog
Ears of rabbits, tail of cat, human's liver, spiders' legs
Witch's mummy, pile of worms, wool of bat, eye of newt
Fenny snake, lizard's leg, eye of cow, tail of a horse
A bottle of blood, pig's nose, hamster's leg
Gall of goat, tooth of wolf,
Double, double toil and trouble
Fire burn, and cauldron bubble.
Scale of dragon, one mouse, one slimy snail shell,
Witch's nose, human's arm, three dogs' heads, pig's lips,
Ditch delivered by a drab
Make the gruel thick and slab.
Add there to a tiger's chawdron
For th' ingredients of our cauldron.

Rosie Richardson (13)
The Holgate Comprehensive School, Hucknall

Witch's Spell

Fenny snake, toe of frog,
Nowlet's wing toenails,
Hair of bat, cat head,
Rat's mummy
Lizard's leg,
Salt-sea shark, human's liver,
Dog tail, tongue of dog.

Wool of bat, tooth of wolf,
Blindworm's sting,
Blaspheming Jew,
Spider's legs, gall of goat,
Rabbit's whiskers,
Cow's eyes.

*Double, double toil and trouble,
Fire burn and cauldron bubble.*

Bird poo and skin of snake,
Witch's nose and scales of hake.

Sarra England (13)
The Holgate Comprehensive School, Hucknall

The Zoo

Listen to the lion growl
And hear the birds which howl
Watch the monkeys running round
Listen to the chipmunks' sound
Then there are zebras drinking from the stream
Listen to the children scream!

Jamie Hufton (11)
The Holgate Comprehensive School, Hucknall

Witch's Spell A Potion To Kill A Man!

Snake's tongue, lizard's skin
And frog's legs, baby owl's head.

These are the first ingredients to make a potion to kill a man!

Ear of dog, skin of rabbit,
Chicken's eye, loads of faggots,
Bird's lungs, rat's tail, smells like a cockatiel.

These are the first ingredients to make a potion to kill a man!

Bat's tooth, cow's heart, horse's lungs,
Pig's legs, head of wolf, caterpillar's body,
Goat's tongue, sheep's nose, camel's foot, elephant's body,
Double, double toil and trouble, fire burn and cauldron bubble.
In poisoned entrails throw.

These are the first ingredients to make a potion to kill a man!

Toad that under cold stone, days and nights has thirty-one sweltered
Venom sleeping got, boils thou first in the charmed pot.
Double, double toil and trouble, fire burn and cauldron bubble.
Fillet of fenny snake, in the cauldron bake,
Eye of newt and toe of frog.

A pair of football socks that have waited to be washed for a week
The sweat from a PE teacher after football training,
Stir it all up and wait for the 2oz of black heads from a teenager.
3oz of rotten eggs that have gone off for at least a week.
We toil it up and wait for bubbles to come and sweep you away.

Daniela Mabbott (14)
The Holgate Comprehensive School, Hucknall

Reyes

Reyes the number nine
He's fast, he's quick
Past a defender in at tick.

He glides, he slides
He crosses, he shoots
The power he uses comes from his boots.

All the fans possess him like treasure
His power, his pace, you cannot measure.

He's only 20, he's very clever
We always will love him
Forever and ever.

His goals he scores are really great
Everyone in the team are all his mates.

He's cheerful he's happy
And all the fans agree
He kicks the ball with a swirling spree.

Remember Reyes because he's the lad
The players, the team, are all glad.

Reyes, Reyes
The Spanish wonder
We all love him
As quick as thunder.

Harry Share (12)
The Holgate Comprehensive School, Hucknall

Rooney!

Rooney's number one
He's worth a tonne
Nobody can beat the Wayne
Because Rooney's got all the fame
Go Wayne, go Wayne.

He's moved to Man Utd for the best
Let him beat all the rest
He scores the goals for the team
As all the crowd scream!

In England he's number one
In the papers and the news
Beckham and Rooney play their best
To beat the rest.

The crowd scream and scream
Singing the England theme.

He's moved to Man Utd for the best
Let him beat all the rest
He scores the goals for the team
As all the crowd scream.

He's fast, he's good!
He's full of mud!
He's only young
But worth a tonne!

Anya Smith (12)
The Holgate Comprehensive School, Hucknall

Lion

Lions lying lazily and lolling in the lush overgrown grass
Lions creeping and crawling to capture their prey
Lions relaxing in the roasting sun
Lions toying and tackling with their prey
Lions calling and crying for lost children to come back
Lions training tactically, ready for when prey comes again.

Kyle Winfield (11)
The Holgate Comprehensive School, Hucknall

The Ballad Of Robin Hood

There was a man who lived in Sherwood
His hideout was in the major oak,
His name was Robin Hood,
And he didn't do what he should.

The evil king wanted to be even richer
He was very greedy indeed.
Whilst he was getting richer,
People were forced to the streets.

The king raised the taxes,
Which Robin didn't like
So he picked up an axe
And pinched the tax back.

He shared it out between the poor,
They moved back into their houses,
And weren't poor anymore.
But the king wasn't very happy about that

The king sent out for Robin Hood
But never found him in Sherwood
For not doing what he should
So he carried on stealing but never got caught.

Kyle Thomas (12)
The Holgate Comprehensive School, Hucknall

What I See

W ailing children
H ats made out of straw
A nimals with big, sharp claws
T alking parents in the park

I cing melting in the sun.

S leeping cats in the grass
E verybody having picnics
E veryone having fun.

Daniel Bullin (11)
The Holgate Comprehensive School, Hucknall

The One I Care About

I really love thee it's hard to explain,
For the things that I feel
But it's just the pain.

I will let the pain carry on forever,
'Cos if the pain wasn't there
Then we don't love each other.

I miss you loads when you're not there
But I miss you even more
When you are there.

I go to sleep holding your bear at night
I toss and turn
But still I'm hugging it tight.

I will never let you go
'Cos I love you so
But just to let you know
We've still got room to grow.

Louise Bailey (15)
The Holgate Comprehensive School, Hucknall

The Song Of LJ

I'm a power-mad girl; I'm a rune finder
When I've found what I want, I become kinder.
I'm a warrior princess,
I killed the Loch Ness.
I'm a point guard; I'm the net,
I will score so place a bet.
I'm a movie star on the big screen,
If you ditch me I will make a scene.
I'm a witch; I'll do a spell,
If you cross me I'll send you to Hell.
For I am the best, I am the one.
The witch who can deflect a gun.

Lauri Jo Dennis (12)
The Holgate Comprehensive School, Hucknall

Hate

I really hate you. You are very weird
Your face looks like glue. You've got a stupid beard
I think you really smell. You live in a cupboard or maybe a well.
Your face should be covered
Most people really hate you. You walk like a candle
You haven't got a shoe. Your face is a mangle.
So get out of here or go buy some beer
You give people the flu. You walk around the street
When they look at you eating some horrible raw meat
You say hello to everybody, wish you had a friend
But you are so snobby, everybody goes round the bend
You should be a cleaner, go, and buy yourself a brush
You shouldn't be any merrier, so go cut a thorn bush
You have not got money, to buy some bee honey.

Fraser Pearson (13)
The Holgate Comprehensive School, Hucknall

The Rabbit In The Mixer

The bunny went through the mixer
And came out all complete
He was shivering all over
And covered in concrete.

The poor little bunny
Got soaked with water
And all the builders were making
Was a great big pile of mortar.

He was inside the concrete
In the merry month of May,
The builders cleaned him up
And then he ran away.

Octavia Wisbey (12)
The Holgate Comprehensive School, Hucknall

Taking Chances!

Did you ever love someone and know they didn't care?
Did you ever look into someone's eyes and sing a little song?
Did you ever look into someone's heart, wishing you were there?
Did you ever go one day, and think that's far too long?

You cry at night and almost go insane
Nothing in this world causes so much pain
I just don't understand, you always complain
Why do you always act so lame?

If I could choose between love and death
I'd think I'd rather die
All I need to do, is take one breath
And take a second try.

Love hurts and the price is high
So I say 'Don't fall in love' because it'll hurt before you know.
Before you know it you'll be crying
So let's just be friends, just turn and go.

Natalie Arme (14)
The Holgate Comprehensive School, Hucknall

The Ballad Of The Rabbit In The Mixer

There was a little rabbit,
A rabbit in a mixer,
Swirled and scooped around,
A terrified little creature.

Smothered in tons of sand,
Swirled with gallons of water,
Swept to a machine with hammers,
A bit like rabbit slaughter.

It crawled itself free
Rescued by a man,
Who cleaned it up and dried it,
And then away it ran.

Katie Hough (12)
The Holgate Comprehensive School, Hucknall

Where Is Elle?

Where is Elle, Mum?
Where is Elle?
Maybe she's in the garden,
Or maybe near the telly.

Is she in the bathroom?
Is she in the shed?
Is she in the hallway, Mum?
Or is she still in bed?

Has she gone down town, Mum?
Or is she near the PC?
Is she in the kitchen, Mum?
No, I bet she's with ET!

Is she in her bedroom, Mum?
Or is she under the table?
I think she's in her cupboard, Mum?
No, I think she's in the stable.

I don't know where she is, Mum?
Please can you help me?
Where is Elle, Mum?
Where is Elle?

Holly Spencer (12)
The Holgate Comprehensive School, Hucknall

The Sea

The sea roars like a lion,
The sea whispers like a mouse,
The sea crashes like colliding cars against the cliffs,
The sea taps like water dripping from taps,
The sea leaps like a cricket jumping in the grass.

Daniel Evans (11)
The Holgate Comprehensive School, Hucknall

The Rabbit In The Mixer

I fell into a quarry
And was scooped up with some sand.
I was found on top of a concrete block
Shivering all around.

I had been mixed around with water
Then I was starting to cry.
I was hammered down into a block
Before I was allowed to dry.

I fell into a quarry
It was ages before I was found
Then eventually
I was home, safe and sound.

Hannah McConnell (12)
The Holgate Comprehensive School, Hucknall

Witches' Spells

We put in out of date milk,
Then we add sick and poo.
And human eyes and brain,
Then lungs and heart out of a human.
Put in 100 ants and cut-off fingers
Then add in horses poo and half of a human.
Now cut a human head off.
Stir snails and burn them on the fire,
Put in snake and cut it in bites.
Stir it together and add bat's wings and head
Always add hot chilli peppers and cat.

Simon Greensmith (13)
The Holgate Comprehensive School, Hucknall

Spell Ingredients

Eyeball of an ass
Skin of a dead antelope
Blood from a newborn baby
Baby's sick
Mud that has horse pee on it
Manure from a cow
The ears of a pig
Sour, sweaty armpits.

*Double, double cauldron bubble stir around
And let's make trouble!*

The guts of a hyena
A lot of snails
A lot of nails
A mouldy egg
Mouldy teeth
Snacks, forks.

*Double, double cauldron bubble stir around
And let's make trouble!*

Dale Cotterill (13)
The Holgate Comprehensive School, Hucknall

The Zoo

T igers growling behind the bars
H yena's laughing, oh what a sight
E lephants stomping oh what a fright.

Z ebras, stripy like the crossing on the road
O wls are hooting, feathers soft to the touch
O tters diving, twisting and turning.

Megan Lynch (11)
The Holgate Comprehensive School, Hucknall

Witch's Spell

For my potion I will need:
Maggot guts, really rotten, reeking with a terrible smell!
And throw in some skin of a rabbit scraped off the M1.
All double, double toil and trouble;
Fire burn and cauldron bubble.
Half a pound of mouldy mouse droppings,
Half a pound of aged bogies!
Mouldy pies from the school canteen,
Then the dripping of sweat of a PE teacher's armpit.
All double, double toil and trouble;
Fire burn and cauldron bubble.
Mouldy toenail clippings from Mr Lee's feet
Pus of an oozing boil.
A rotten, crusty, month-old sock just found from under your bed,
Smelling rotten horse poo with flies all over it,
Mouldy creamy milk just coming out of a cut open cow,
Then throw is some cows' udders.
All double, double toil and trouble;
Fire burn and cauldron bubble.
My mum's horrible dinners
That has just been pulled out of a bin by a tramp,
The guts of a owlet that's just been ripped up into threads by a cat,
A rotten horrible disease carrying rats' entrails,
And for the special ingredients, a teacher.

Kyle Lester (13)
The Holgate Comprehensive School, Hucknall

Russia

I go to school to learn
The teachers go to earn
3 days in
3 days out.

Men come in one by one
Gun by gun
Bang by bang
Cry by cry.

It's hard not to scream
But they're coming.

Men come in one by one
Gun by gun
Bang by bang
Cry by cry.

We run for the fire door
Knowing I'll see no more
There they are
Men in front
Men behind
This is the end.

Jessica Wheatley (12)
The Holgate Comprehensive School, Hucknall

Rabbit In The Mixer

'Tell us a story Grandad,'
The bunny rabbits implored,
'About the block of concrete
Out of which you clawed.'

The old adventure smiled
And waved a wrinkled paw,
'All right children settle down
I'll tell it just one more time.

I was just a baby rabbit
And I walked on a construction site
I got scooped up in sand
I thought I was never going to get out, it was very tight.

I was lucky it did not set
But I could not move
I thought I would never escape
But I did, there is no doubt.

I clawed away
In the concrete there was a hole
I was lucky I got out
I saw a mole.

He said, 'I will help you.'
He got me out of there,
Now we are best of friends
Now I will never go back there, not even if it is a dare!'

Matt Clifton (12)
The Holgate Comprehensive School, Hucknall

The Baby!

Steve and Karen
Ain't got no baby
But that don't mean
He ain't got no lady.

They tried once
They tried twice
And ended up
Having mice.

Steve and Karen
Ain't got no baby
But that don't mean
Steve ain't got no lady

But Karen's going
To think twice
About those pet mice
And went to the doctors for some advice.

When Karen found out
She was upset
And ended up putting Steve
In a net and she gave Tracey a threat.

Ellis Gormley (12)
The Holgate Comprehensive School, Hucknall

The Ballad Of Wayne Rooney!

He went from Everton to Man U
He's the greatest footballer of all
Only 18 years old
The most famous of them all.

The supporters of Man U are
Proud to give their support
He is extremely skilled and
Talented in this sport.

His hat-tricks shocking the crowd
And all you can hear is the crowd shouting loud
Before you know he's scored a goal
He's running around the pitch
With the crowd shouting loud.

He gets the ball again and
He makes his way to the goal
And he scores again and
He runs round the pitch with joy.

When the final whistle blows
And they have won
He walks off the pitch with a smile on his face
And the crowd shouting a loud.

Rebecca Thorley (12)
The Holgate Comprehensive School, Hucknall

I Hate The Way You . . .

I hate the way you broke my heart,
I hate the way you made me feel when we fell apart,
The way you sat and cried at night,
And the way we always had a fight,
But I still hate the way that we're not together
And the way I thought it would last forever,
But now I know how true love felt,
And it hurts as much as being hit by a belt.

Toni French (14)
The Holgate Comprehensive School, Hucknall

Spell Ingredients

A potion to make you smaller
Spit from an ass.
Nose of a dead cow.
Earwax from a rat.

*Double, double toil and trouble
Fire burn and cauldron bubble.*

Blood from a newborn baby.
Eyeballs from a dead dog.
8 rotten eggs
Teeth from a dead rabbit
Cheesy sock from a man that has not changed them for 28 weeks
Dog poo from 8 weeks ago.

Travis Prew (13)
The Holgate Comprehensive School, Hucknall

The Lonely City

Bright lights shine through the misty night
There is a wisp of fright
A blue siren on a car
The noise travels wide and far.

Surrounded by an angry crowd
The fallen skyscraper once stood tall and proud.

The air is dirty, dull and humid
Office buildings are as tall as pyramids
And the thing I liked best of all
Was the skyscraper standing proud and tall.

There is debris everywhere
Nothing survived, not even a hair
Emergency services rushed to the scene.

The people who did this must be incredibly mean
'Why did they do it?' families cry
We will never know
Why they wanted them to die.

Adrian Dean (11)
The Lakelands School, Ellesmere

The Prison Cells Of New York

All alone in the New York night,
But sheltered from the cold,
Scared and what a fright,
Being against the truth I told.

All alone in the New York night,
Far from the rush of cars,
Waiting hours and hours for the moon to rise,
Behind the steel bars.

All alone in the New York night,
Getting older each day,
The man who killed my friend,
Is the man that's going to pay.

All alone in the New York night,
Trapped beneath the stars,
For a crime I didn't commit,
Still imprisoned inside the metal bars.

All alone in the New York night,
Ten more years to bear,
Face to face with the outside world,
For them all to look and stare.

Jackie Jones (11)
The Lakelands School, Ellesmere

Rival's Thoughts

I sway like a blade of grass in the wind,
As I am cut down like a tethered dog,
The great warrior I once was,
Sinks like a very battered ship,
I loosen my grip on my sword,
As I slowly drift out of memory and life . . .
My heart beats slower,
As darkness overtakes my eyes,
The sun has set on my time,
And has risen as a new face in the holy land,
Ha! He thought he could overcome the power of me?
The world's best fighter?

He was wrong!
Not even the person who taught
Me could stand a chance.

No one can destroy me,
Everyone who tries to oppose me,
Will fight like dogs,
And die like dogs,
I'm invincible.

William Martin (11)
The Lakelands School, Ellesmere

Monsters Everywhere

There are monsters in the cupboard,
There are monsters in the pipes,
But worst of them is the Brolathan,
He will creep under the floorboards.

There are monsters in the light bulbs,
There are monsters in the drawers,
But the worst is the Brolathan,
Who turns out all the lights.

There are monsters in the wires,
There are monsters under the beds,
But the worst is the Brolathan,
Who grabs you and . . . *arrghhhhhhhhhhhhhhhh!*

Henry Traynor (12)
The Lakelands School, Ellesmere

Bakery

Mum is baking in the kitchen
I can smell the lovely hot cross buns
Baking under the oven like the sun bakes the leaves on a tree
I listen quietly to the food raising
My mouth watering.

Freshly-baked bread on the worktop
The smell creeping through the house
And floating up your nose.

I love living in a bakery
I get loads of food for free
But if you think that I can cook
You've got to be crazy!

Joe Hatton (11)
The Lakelands School, Ellesmere

Stormy Days

Stormy days cowering in the house,
It is no longer as quiet as a mouse.

Stormy days hiding in my room,
Because outside it's a world of doom.

The world closing in,
Round and round it goes.

Flashing, flashing everywhere,
Splitting the sky with a great tear.

*Boom, boom, boom it goes,
Zigzag zap, zigzag zap.*

Crash, bang, boom,
Goes the thunder.

Lightning
Crashing to the ground.

The sunny days playing down the road,
Gone. It's all a big blur.

Why is this happening?
I wonder why.

Stormy days hiding in the house,
It is no longer as quiet as a mouse.

Stormy days hiding in my room,
Because outside it's a world of doom.

Becky Jeffrey (12)
The Lakelands School, Ellesmere

Was This The . . . ?

Was this the bedroom that you died in?
Lonely, dusty and dark.
Where curtains hang on the bloodied rail
And the towel stained so badly
Like your heart.

Are they the pictures you drew?
You felt depressed
With your head in your hands.
The chair of doom
Like your brain.

Was this the window you looked through?
Clouded with dust
As I rub the dust off
And see the plain view I see
Just like you!

Louise Norris (11)
The Lakelands School, Ellesmere

Why?

Why can't the world be black and white?
Why can't it be clear what's wrong and right?
Why can't the world be crystal clear?
Why won't people listen to what they hear?
Why does the world love to hate?
Why do we panic if we arrive late?
Why does the world argue and shout?
Why don't we calmly sort it out?
Why can't the world be somewhere safe?
Why can't we make it a happier place?
Why does the world cheat and lie?
Why one is born another one dies?
Why?

Katie Freeman (14)
The Long Eaton School, Long Eaton

My Mate

You make me laugh, you make me smile,
You help me out and you're there all the while,
To be there to talk to me, for you're a true friend,
And I will be there for you until the end.

You're a strong team leader and the greatest mate,
Ask anyone around, you're really great!
Everyone likes you, you've got not one enemy,
You're a really great friend, can't you see?

You're always there, just for a chat,
Or a friendly laugh, you're always up for that,
But now you've changed,
What happened to you?
Why can't we talk like we always used to?

I cling to the memories,
Now that you say that you don't care,
What happened to the times,
When you used to be there?

Rachel Sloper (12)
The Long Eaton School, Long Eaton

Night Is!

Night is a coal-black blanket
Night is lit-up stars that twinkle in the night sky
Night is a yellow, glistening moon
Night is the home where loved ones passed away
Night is full of fearful, frightening sounds
Night is when innocent children cry
Night is when fluffy clouds of dreams fill the dark sky
Night is a happening moment
Night is full of gruesome bugs and terrifying creatures
Night is like a pitch-black room
Night is when hideous monsters come alive
Night is full of dread and doom.

Gemma Pickering (13)
The Long Eaton School, Long Eaton

Horrendous Hurricane

Sugar-coated toffee, pink iced cakes,
The delicious smell a tasty hot dog makes.
Dragonflies hum and lemonade fizzes,
On the hot beach you might see some lizards.
Football shirts covered with the number seven,
Chocolate ice cream tastes like perfect Heaven.

Wind picks up, spots of rain,
I think it could be the horrendous hurricane.
No more picnics, no more fun,
No more playing, no more sun.
Everyone's running, getting away,
In the hope of it lasting for one dull day.

Rain is slowing, everything's changed,
The beach is full up once again.
The dragonflies are humming, the lemonade fizzes,
Out back come all of the lizards.
It was terribly terrifying when it came,
Now say goodbye to the horrendous hurricane.

Josh Allsop (13)
The Long Eaton School, Long Eaton

Before I Die . . .

Before I die I want to do a lot,
Climb Everest right up to the top,
Travel the world in 80 days,
Live my life in many ways.

Undo the lies, untie the knots,
Let people know I loved them lots,
Not be scared, confront my fears,
Think of memories through past years.

As I think what could have been,
Say sorry to those to whom I've been mean,
Undo the rifts, foe to friend,
Live my life right through to the end.

Jemma Shaw (13)
The Long Eaton School, Long Eaton

Love Is . . .

Love is a bunch of blooming flowers,
Opening for all to see,
Love is a word of comfort,
Just for you and me.
Love is a priceless piece of treasure,
Gleaming into my eyes,
Love is a twinkling star,
The sparkle never dies.
Love is a deep, dark secret,
Waiting for us to share,
Love is another charming soul,
Someone else who genuinely cares.
Love is an enchanting thought,
Deep inside your head,
Love is a dream, a fantasy,
Silent words that are never said.
Love is many things: family, friends and home.
Love is knowing you are safe, warm and never alone.

Abby Mycroft (13)
The Long Eaton School, Long Eaton

At Dawn

I watch myself, no longer pink and warm
But white and cold, it's approaching dawn.
It's my funeral and I'm not there
To share the fruits of my life so fair.
They grin and guffaw and think about me
The places I've been and the places I'd be.
I glance at my mum and she's not quite as sad
Because during my first years, she treated me bad.
I look at my dad as he smiles in vain
But deep inside I know he feels pain.
I watch myself, no longer pink and warm
But white and cold as it ticks just past dawn.

Matthew Debbage (14)
The Long Eaton School, Long Eaton

Gone

A lonely tear rolled down my cheek tonight,
As he had gone to God's delight,
Up in the clouds so far away,
I want him here and here to stay.

I touched his heart and heard him say,
'I will love you now and for every day.'
But how will he love me when he's not here?
That's the only part which is unfair and unclear.

My heart is empty and my mind is blank,
The long-lost memories there, now have sank,
My true love for him will never vanish
Even though, to Heaven, he has now been banished.

A lonely tear rolled down my cheek tonight,
I stared at him in my dream's delight,
I held him tight and held him close,
But he slipped away just like a ghost.

Holly Kemish (13)
The Long Eaton School, Long Eaton

The Mermaid

The sun is beating down upon golden sands,
Children and adults alike laugh and play in the sparkling sea.
A silent and beautiful creature splashes away from the shore,
And scoops up her long tail onto a smooth rock.
She sighs as she watches families having fun on land,
Wishing that she could run around like them.
The wind whistles through her long, fair hair,
Whipping it lightly across her tanned shoulders.
A young boy glances up from his sandcastle for a moment,
Just in time to see a glossy rainbow-patterned tail,
Disappear deep into the ocean of silvery blue.
The reflection of the setting sun ripples out onto the shore,
Which is now as empty and silent as the surface of the moon,
The gentle crash of the waves echoes through the sleeping town.

Laura Codrington (12)
The Long Eaton School, Long Eaton

No, Never

The house now feels so empty.
No card tricks anymore.
No waving through the window
As he enters through the door.

No oil on his hands from work.
No glasses I loved to try.
Never the one last meeting.
No chance to say goodbye.

No jokes to make me giggle.
No jokes to make me laugh.
No more help with homework.
No goodbye I long to have.

The house now feels so empty.
The goodbye I'll forever long.
No, never the one last meeting
Now that my grandad's gone.

Emma Riley (14)
The Long Eaton School, Long Eaton

Winter

The freezing frost crawls across the glistening ground,
Covering the floor like an icy carpet,
It pounces on trees like a stalking panther,
Leaving them lifeless and bare,
It charges across the land like a rampant rhino,
It whistles like a sweet-singing wren,
It spits out rain like a vicious cobra,
It roars down the streets like a giant lion,
The blazing sun comes out, the lonely clouds die,
Winter has finally disappeared.

Craig White (13)
The Long Eaton School, Long Eaton

A Face Stares Back

She looks in the mirror
A face stares back
The face of a killer
Her eyes are pitch-black.

She looks in the water
A face stares back
It's the face of her daughter
Who lies dead in the sack.

She looks in the window
A face stares back
It's the face of her mother
Who never came back.

She looks at the picture
She sees a scarred cheek
It's the fist of her father
Who makes her mind weak.

Catherine McLaughlin (14)
The Long Eaton School, Long Eaton

A Thing Called Love

Love is a mug of marshmallow-topped hot chocolate,
A spectacular snowy-white dove crooning in my apple tree.

Love is a new Sims game for my PC,
A roast beef lunch made by me.

Love is a massive surprise for me,
A book by Jacqueline Wilson that's a little funny.

Love is a the angel Dad made for me,
A colourful sunset that's great to see,
Downtown with a purse full of precious money.

This is what love is for me.

Katie Clayton (12)
The Long Eaton School, Long Eaton

Last Thoughts Of A Prisoner Of War

They blindfold us now,
As we're strapped to a pole,
They load their sordid weapons,
Do they have no soul?

I hear a loud shout,
My time has now come,
Thirteen of us left now,
Unlucky for some.

He orders them now,
To shoot us all,
I pray to the heavens,
God, please hear my desperate call.

I am going to be killed now,
Of this I am sure,
The end of my life,
As a prisoner of war.

James Glover (14)
The Long Eaton School, Long Eaton

At The Fairground

Candyfloss, candyfloss,
I love to eat lots and lots.
Toffee apples are so sticky,
Very sweet, but not sickly.
Burgers, chips, covered in grease,
Can I have more ketchup please?
Sweets, chocolates, cakes and all,
I think I hear my stomach call.
The roller coaster goes so quick!
I've eaten too much, I feel sick!

Amy Platkiw (13)
The Long Eaton School, Long Eaton

Ian

The day you left and went away,
Was the day I was meant to cry.
The day you left and went away,
Was the day I said goodbye.

The day you left and went away,
I cried for hours, endless days.
The day you left and went away,
I dealt with emotion in different ways.

The day you left and went away,
Our family got closer, more of a team.
The day you left and went away,
My heart was bursting at the seam.

The day you left and went away,
Was the day I had to cry.
The day you left and went away,
Was the day I had to say goodbye.

When I look back at the good times we had,
It makes me realise there's no need to be sad.
As the years go by my heart opens wide,
Which means there's more room for you inside.

What I'm trying to say is we miss you, ya know,
Although he didn't warn us that you had to go.
It's clear now that God believes you are the one,
It's clear to me now that's why you are gone.

Jade Sheppard (14)
The Long Eaton School, Long Eaton

World War One Life In The Trenches

I am on the English side,
Will we win or will we die?
Will it be a vicious fight?
We will use all our might.

We live in trenches dirty and old,
Filled with things and very cold.
Mice and rats, lice and fleas,
Are always running around our knees.

The toilets are just a hole,
Would prefer to use a bowl.
Toss it over the top of the trench,
Never mind the smelly stench.

My feet are swelling in the heat,
As the sun shines down on a beat.
More water we need to keep us fit,
I wish I could get out of this dirty pit.

I am here from day to day,
It should be me next, I pray.
People die every day on top of the wire,
Could they die any higher?

I am on the English side,
Will we win or will we die?
Will it be a vicious fight?
We will use all our might.

Siân Groves (13)
The Long Eaton School, Long Eaton

The Sea

The calm sea lapping on the seashore
The gentle breeze whipping up the waves
Quietly whispering, gently whistling
Shimmering, glimmering, trembling, glistening.

The seagulls shrieking high above
The sea that shakes far below
Gently quivering, slowly shivering
Shushing, hushing, gushing, flushing.

But now the stormy sea tears apart the seashore
The cruel wind whizzing round and round
Hurriedly clashing, nastily bashing
Clapping, slapping, clattering, shattering.

The seagulls scream out a warning
Of evil seas gobbling up the shore
Loudly roaring, fearfully snoring
Smashing, dashing, flashing, lashing.

Michelle Newbold (13)
The Long Eaton School, Long Eaton

The Cola Bottle's Whip

It fizzes and fuzzes
And wraps its sour whip around my innocent tongue.
It bumps. It hits you then you chew.
It breaks up into little bits.
It grinds, it winds, it blows my mind.
They all go in one at a time.
Then I break my tradition and two go in together.
They buzz and stick.
My teeth pull them apart and I get straight to the heart.
I've hit the cola bit.
The intense flavour splits open and fills my body.
I twist and turn and run around,
Then it's gone.
No more left until next time.

Scott Twells (13)
The Long Eaton School, Long Eaton

At A Motocross Championship

Rumbling engines rattle and hum
The crowd laughing at the motorists falling
Lights glowing over the audience.

People booming barks of laughter
Loud music bouncing off the wall
Cheering, moaning and loud groans.

Rumbling engines rattle and hum
The crowd laughing at the motorists falling
Lights glowing over the audience.

Sizzling hot dogs being eaten
Girls giggling at sexy riders
Lads clapping at the cool tricks.

Rumbling engines rattle and hum
The crowd laughing at the motorists falling
Lights glowing over the audience.

The audience choking on bike fumes
Bikers praying and shuddering
Then they crash into the barriers.

Rumbling engines rattle and hum
The crowd laughing at the motorists falling
Lights glowing over the audience.

Robert Porter (12)
The Long Eaton School, Long Eaton

The Sea

The sea is a starving animal, alone and worried.
Its claws grab the air and pulls it into its icy chest.
The sea is a barbarian, wild and uncivilised
As it clashes against its wild friends.
Its Arctic skin overlapped the sandy shore.
The shells were swallowed by the sea's wide and open mouth.
Its blue coat reached out its hand and snatched away the sand.

Serena Metcalfe (13)
The Long Eaton School, Long Eaton

The Firework Display

Boom, bang, whoosh
Fly the fireworks high
Higher and higher the fireworks fly.

Sprinkle, twinkle
Way up high
Bright, bold colours
Away they fly.

Boom, bang, whoosh
Fly the fireworks high
Higher and higher the fireworks fly.

Louder and louder
Bang, bang, bang
High in the sky
Way they clang.

Boom, bang, whoosh
Fly the fireworks high
Higher and higher the fireworks fly.

Brittany Woodhouse (12)
The Long Eaton School, Long Eaton

The Way The Wind Blows

Gentle as a lover's kiss,
Raging as a mad, black bull,
Sweetly as a blackbird's song,
The wind can be them all.

Taking hats and frightening cats,
As they scream and blunder.
The softest whistle blows the clouds,
Autumn leaves fall asunder.
In the desert, hairdryer hot,
Snowstorms blown to drifting,
Inside out brollies struggle hard,
The wind is their master.

Sarah Francis (12)
The Long Eaton School, Long Eaton

Jack Frost

A tall thin man with a frozen nose
Swiftly through winter, quietly he goes.

With a frost-bitten face chilled to the bone
Sitting in his ice house all on his own.

Anything he touches he instantly freezes
But sledging children he always pleases.

With spiky joints and pointed fingers
Wherever he goes, a bitter wind still lingers.

As the snow melts and winter ends
Jack bids goodbye to all his friends.

Springtime comes; it's getting near
Jack retreats for the rest of the year.

Ryan Walker (12)
The Long Eaton School, Long Eaton

Chains

As I lie so still, so silent
I try to escape, free my mind from the tyrant.
I look out the window, I can see
A bird flying by, so close to me.
I look at the world, not mine anymore
Because I am a prisoner, stranded at my core.
I am a prisoner of my mind, so alone,
I am not free, I cannot roam
But I know deep inside, my bird still flies,
Even if my heart still cries.
For you broke the chains for me, made me free
But now you've gone, so there's no you, just me!

Ashley Matthews (13)
The Long Eaton School, Long Eaton

Trenches

I laid my head against the mud,
My thoughts were far away.
The shells were ringing in my ear,
On this damp and dismal day.
'Wake up, old son,' the sergeant cried,
I moved and turned my head.
'If you don't move your butt, my lad,
You'll end up being dead.'
I tried to move my heavy feet,
But found it very hard.
My ankles were so swollen,
My elbows burnt and tarred.
For two days now I'd looked at him,
My friend called Tommy Cox.
Poor chap, he took it in the head,
I think I'll take his socks.
I turned to face my sergeant,
His face was full of fright.
The enemy were still firing,
We fought with all our might.
Nightfall came, the shells died down,
We tried to get some sleep.
This godforsaken hellhole,
So dark, damp and deep.
The rats were chewing through my socks,
As I awoke next day.
Was it the lice that made me itch
As my mind began to stray?
If we survive this battle,
And remove this awful stench,
I'll sit one day and remember,
My warfare in the trench!

Anna Smith (14)
The Long Eaton School, Long Eaton

Hostile Environments Poem!

White, foggy mountains,
Hazardous, blistering winds,
Standing way up high.

Rocky, rough rocks,
Waiting to be climbed slowly,
To reach the snow top.

Scorching, rayed desert,
Sombre, yellow, hostile land,
Beaming rays of heat.

Hot, sweaty body,
Lifeless, motionless land,
Mirages occur.

Trembling, cold tundra,
Further off the equator,
The colder it gets.

Shivering coldness,
Icy, blistering frostbite,
Eats away your toes.

Noisy rainforests,
Are very much in danger,
Also animals.

Rain falls down quickly,
In the Amazon jungle,
You will get drenched fast.

Tom Gatehouse (12)
The Long Eaton School, Long Eaton

The Trenches

The freezing cold men lay shivering in their trenches
Listening to the guns, their drumming thunder roll
Leaping to kill mostly every soul.

The rats are stealing all the food
For every pulse their heart does feel
It makes them think like cold steel.

Perish the thoughts of hope and glory
It's all replaced with blood and despair
This is not at all very fair.

For the whole of the land dwells with the stabbing blade
As it did in the days of old
We sit there in despair, blood-sodden and shivering cold.

We thought it was Judgement Day
We sat upright, while drearisome
I lay down again half dead, half living
Wondering, *will the world be sane again?*

Callum Whaley (13)
The Long Eaton School, Long Eaton

The Snake's Warning

Keep away! Keep away!
My tongue means painful death.
I hide under rocks to await my prey.
Keep away! Keep away!
A coil of power I have.
I may not have legs but I'm fast at twirling.
From a tree I hang around the lake.
So watch out! Watch out! I'm always awake.

Sophie Hesketh (12)
The Long Eaton School, Long Eaton

Humanity

Amongst the concrete jungle's trees
Humanity moves with ease
Great innovations of society
Fanatic electronic piety
This is the evolution
Of intelligence.

This great society bears art and culture
Dance, art, music, verse;
Philosophies of the universe
Expression of spirituality
A sense of common decency.

But is this show on the news?
The holocaust of the Jews
Immigrants in camps of cess
People biting the hand that fed them
Society led by politic bedlam
Dictators on the people tread
Ruling by tyrannical dread
Parties talk of the people
But a dictatorship they assemble
Is this the world of artistic freedom?
Is this the world of the people?
Society will always be
But of the people?
We will see.

Angus Martin (16)
The Marches School, Oswestry

Unafraid

Eerie silence wanders all around,
My knees collapse - I fall without a sound,
The darkness opens up again before me,
Swallowing the last of this that I intend to see,
I find no fear inside - merely regret,
I think, for soon I know I will forget.

I look back fondly - only now I do remember,
What was shared, what we did and saw, together.

How carelessly we played,
Unafraid,
The leafy shrine on which we laid,
The river through we'd come to wade,
Unafraid,
The field, the trees, and caves we'd claimed,
The shores where promises were made,
A debt in heart that must be paid,
Your eyes were full of hope, expectation,
As deep and full as those pools of jade,
My own now clouded as my vision fades.

The years we had were bliss although so few,
Young, carefree and innocent before we knew,
That foreign fear and suffering, seen only on the news,
Could happen to us too.

Nothing lives and nothing lasts forever,
And now my final link with you I sever,
I have no will nor means to carry on,
I'm not the last, I'm not the only one.

I know nothing of the path that lies ahead,
But I shall remember what it was you always said,
And though I'm now beyond your mortal aid,
I face my journey ready,
Unafraid.

Alex Winfield (16)
The Marches School, Oswestry

Lost Soul

Could you believe a boy in today's society to live as
A lost soul?
Could you believe a boy brought up with care could be
A lost soul?

But I tell you that such a boy exists
A being of anger, hate and anguish
Just another satanic vessel
With a spirit doomed for his abusal.

To be found on the face of this such boy
Is never a smile, laugh or hint of joy
Some say a lack of love to be sin
But feelings as this are non-existent to him.

But whence stumble upon a girl one day
So fair as the stars on winter's night
Found he his heart so had to pay
The price of love with anger's might.

But let it be known the danger exempted
When lost soul's love suddenly rejected
Cause greed, hate and fear towards fellow men
Reborn is the anger had been detained.

Now empty shell so full of fury
Rage released this time to be set free
Cause pain and suffering by acts so cruel
By the boy of nothing, another lost soul.

Could you believe a boy in today's society to live as
A lost soul?
Could you believe a boy brought up with care could be
A lost soul?

Robert Manning (15)
The Marches School, Oswestry

The Swings

It's a child's haven
Where they can play
Without a care
I would love to play
But I come when everyone has gone.

I sit on the rusty swing
Leaves fluttering along the ground
The familiar happiness sweeps over me
This is my place
Where my thoughts are free
No more worry
Again I am a child.

I swing gently
To and fro
I too don't care
So quiet, so peaceful
I let my mind go
Only the squeaking of the swing is heard.

Georgina Blay (14)
The Priory School, Shrewsbury

Monsters And Women

We all know that at some time that terrible night will come,
A peaceful passing for many and painful end for some.
Some things exist in that terrible night,
Soulless beings who are shunned by the light.
We call these things vampires, monsters or perhaps the undead,
Pale, frightening beings, even their name fills you with dread.
Look closely, my friend, and it may make you quiver,
If you wish to see a monster, go find a mirror.
For most women do things
That would make even a vampire shiver!

Scott Peever (15)
The Priory School, Shrewsbury

My World

The feeling of peacefulness filling the lonely air,
Escaping from the busy world seems to wash away my fears,
The warm sun glistening in nature's eyes,
Welcoming me to the tranquillity of this new world.
A gentle breeze brushes past me,
Closing my sleepy eyes as it goes.
The scuttling leaves, the singing birds help me feel at one.

The surreal atmosphere brings me time to think
Of the true meanings of life.
No end to time in this world so mesmerising.
All thoughts run through my mind,
And all feelings run through my heart.
I'm alone, but accepted as no one can understand
This feeling that doesn't exist to some.
I lie back as the grass softly comforts me.

Harriet Dineen (14)
The Priory School, Shrewsbury

The Severn

Down by the Severn.
The spiritual way in which the gentle river flows.
Releasing my thoughts.
Skimming smooth, flat rocks, which glide across the still waters.

Allowing me to delve right into my mind,
The sheer silence all around me.
Easing myself off the bench, I wait.
Sensually, I step down to the river.
I slip off my shoes and dip my feet into the cold water.
It feels like a release. A release of my worries.

The deep waters lure me in further.
Water creeping up to reach my knees.
The gloopy mud seeping in-between my toes.
I wonder.

Katie Brearley (14)
The Priory School, Shrewsbury

Flying Through The Air

I buckle up.
I hate taking off,
My stomach churns.
We're off.

As we go through the clouds, it brings back memories.
I remember playing as a boy with my dad
Looking in the sky and clouds
Above any man or being.
The calmness of a plane is invigorating,
The quiet which at any other place would drive you mad
But here you have time for your mind to run wild.
I put on my Walkman,
Now I know I have arrived.

3 hours pass,
I awake from my slumber.
I turn once again to the steamed-up window.
The mesmerising patterns clouds make are outstanding.
I rub my eyes, I feel like I'm floating on air.
God is near.
I feel His presence.
I hardly notice we have landed.

Daniel Pugh (14)
The Priory School, Shrewsbury

Smoker

Here lies a smoker,
Stupid and vain,
Thought he was cool,
Should think again.
Died of cancer at 32,
All his debts still due.
He may have had stained teeth and face,
But don't worry, he looked grown-up and ace.

Charles Andrews (13)
The Priory School, Shrewsbury

A River

The gentle current carried me
On and on
The lazy trout greeting me with a wave of its flipper
The breeze playing across my face, blowing my hair
Taking me up
Up to the clear blue sky
What was the wind? I thought
As I was carried ever on.

The world watched my passing
As a giant would an ant
On I was carried
Ever on
The weed lying in the midday sun
Content whilst being caressed
By the happily bubbling water
As I was carried ever on.

Joseph Sadowski (14)
The Priory School, Shrewsbury

Beauty Within

My lips were like Marmite,
But now they're like jam.
My hair was like straw,
But now I'm lookin' glam.

My eyes were dull as river-brown,
But now they're sparkling, ocean-blue.
When you gaze into them once more,
You'll see a reflection of you.

My persona, once a messed-up girl,
Is now shining full of dreams.
That 'geek' you used to laugh at,
Was never what she seemed.

Zoe Davies (15)
The Priory School, Shrewsbury

A Series Of Unfortunate Events

Trundle along Brinny Beach,
Three Baudeleire's orphans soon to be,
Bundles of misfortune nearing their reach,
As they skip stones out to sea,
Unfortunate.

Mysterious figure in the distance is nearing,
Parent dead, engulfed in fire,
Tear-saturated children can't believe what they're hearing,
Beloved returned is all they desire,
Unfortunate.

Live with the banker, coughing and spluttering,
Itchy garments and bitten-tongue conversation,
Splutter, cough, splutter, tell them they're leaving,
Count Olaf brings an uplifting sensation,
Unfortunate.

Career, a repulsive villain, Count is so greedy,
Deviating a plot to steal the fortune,
Tattoo eye shrouding, burning stare is beady,
Wedding chimes only lead to misfortune,
Unfortunate.

No one takes notice, will not believe,
Upstage Olaf and sign in wrong hand,
Power disconnected, Devil takes his leave,
Baudeleire's relatives on demand,
Unfortunately.

Becky Lea (15)
The Priory School, Shrewsbury

My Summer Holiday

If I were on holiday,
France is where I'd be,
Sitting on the seashore,
Or jumping in the sea.

I may be lying on the beach,
With an ice cream in each hand,
Getting a great suntan,
Or playing in the sand.

Or in the waves bodyboarding,
In the salty water,
With my mum and dad exclaiming,
'What a silly daughter!'

On the other hand out come the clouds,
And the sky is not so blue,
Then suddenly the rain begins to pour,
And there's not much we can do.

So off we trail back to the cottage,
With jigsaw puzzles galore,
Or watching black and white TV,
With two channels or more.

Every holiday's uncertain,
Rain or shine, it's not quite clear,
But one thing *is* for sure,
We will be coming back next year.

Olivia Rossall (13)
The Priory School, Shrewsbury

Don't

Don't shout so loud,
Don't hit my legs,
Don't make me eat my tea,
Don't smack me,
When I stain the carpet,
Just be nice to me.

Don't lock me,
In the bathroom,
Until I've stopped the shouting,
You locked me in,
A whole hour once,
Yes, I was counting.

Don't go out,
Every night,
I cannot get to sleep,
Don't lock me in,
My filthy bedroom,
Quiet and still I'll keep.

Don't go away,
And not come back,
Like you did last week,
I waited and waited,
For days and days,
Through the keyhole I peek.

Don't starve me,
For a whole day,
I feel really ill,
Please don't go,
Inside the cupboard,
And take another pill.

Don't drag me,
Towards the window,
And threaten to throw me over,
I hate it when you,
Come back in,
Definitely not sober.

Don't hit me,
With your belt,
When I call for you,
I wish that you,
Just wouldn't,
Hit my little sister too.

Don't bring back,
All those dodgy people,
Who kick me, call me names,
When you had them round,
Last week I dreaded,
The moment that they came.

Don't come at me,
With the kitchen knife,
It really causes pain,
You scare me so,
Please, please don't,
Do it ever again.

Megan Evans (12)
The Priory School, Shrewsbury

The Ghetto

I'm a survivor who likes to rap;
I drink lemonade with my ginger snaps.
I sit at home and write my rhymes,
Get inspiration from the Sunday Times.
I go to the library to research my art,
In my gangsta crew I play my part.
I drive my bike as fast as you need,
We practise smuggling sunflower seeds.
I once knew a lad who used to smoke;
I get dizzy from drinking Coke.
Me and my crew, we rock hard,
We've all got a library card.
Now it's time to drop this beat,
My homework is still not complete.

Andy Cormack (14)
The Priory School, Shrewsbury

Blue Planet

Darting adumbrates in the mist,
Many together as if they've kissed,
Ducks and dives, turns and twists,
I have amity for our Blue Planet.

A looming shadow overhead,
The sharks are here, they want to be fed,
The army of the dead it is said,
I have amity for our Blue Planet.

Fish with such lubricate flippers,
Birds with feet which look like slippers,
Exquisite gliders like a kipper,
I have amity for our Blue Planet.

A frightful darkness surrounds the sea,
Altering it for human needs,
These creatures die because of thee,
I have amity for our Blue Planet.

An abstruse district lies below,
What lies down there? You will never know,
Creatures of beauty, that just shows,
Why I have amity for our Blue Planet.

Joe Travis (12)
The Priory School, Shrewsbury

The Snow Did Fall In August

I was upstairs cleaning the basement,
For my mum whose beard is brown.
When my dad, who is an actress,
Came in and smiled with a frown.

The cat was barking loudly,
And the birds all sang, *'Ring, ring,'*
And since the snow did fall in August,
The flowers began to sing.

Grace Thompson (13)
The Priory School, Shrewsbury

The Fates

The Fates are gruesome,
With only one eye between them.
They are old and grey.
They see the future,
And will tell you for a price.
They see the past, the present.
Everything happening in the world is under their eye.
They have one tooth between them.
They are bitter, they are old.
They have existed from the beginning of time.
They hold the fabric of life.
They sank Atlantis.
They conducted World War 2,
And laughed at Pearl Harbour.
They destroy our dreams.
They are the bringers of hate and anger.
They cause hope and love.
They hold our fate within their withered hands.
They hold the thread of life.
They have the scissors of death.
They are pain, they are death.
They are disease, they are destiny.
They are the Grey Ones.
They are The Fates.

Holly Edwards (13)
The Priory School, Shrewsbury

The Earth

The sun, the sea, the sand, the soil.
It all makes up one thing.
Something that's part of you and me.
The bird, the bush, the tree.
The Earth is what we call it.
Our priceless, humble home.
It's where our race will carry on forever and a day.

Emily Bidder (13)
The Priory School, Shrewsbury

It Was An Accident

I didn't mean to knock it on the floor
Or get fingerprints on the door
That's why now I'm in my room
Mum should let me out soon.

What's that? Why is it there?
It's too high for me, it's up in the air
It's that thing Mum told me never to touch
But it's so shiny, I like it so much.

I'm standing on my brand new chair
Trying to reach up in the air
Yes, I've got it, it's in my hand
I've just taken it from the stand.

I get my best paints out
It'll look better so Mum won't shout
Some pink here, some red and brown there
A flower and a car, a cuddly big bear.

'Look, Mum, look what I've done,
It's a car and a big, shiny sun,
I thought your ornament was very boring,
So I painted on it, my best drawing!'

Natalie Watkins (12)
The Priory School, Shrewsbury

The Unwanted Creature

He struggled to move across the room
His full weight leaning on the broom.
The bristles scratched the hard, polished floor
The old man limped towards the door.

The door creaked open, not by demand
He turned around to see a hand.
The old man raised the broom above his head
Leaving the unwanted creature dead.

Kelly Beesty (13)
The Priory School, Shrewsbury

The Tale Of Henry Hash

Horrid Henry Hash
Ate too much bangers and mash.
He grew like a huge balloon,
His mother cried,
His father sighed,
As he took up most of the room.

Horrid Henry Hash
Hit the ceiling with a crash.
Henry's head broke through the roof,
His grandma groaned,
His grandpa moaned,
As they realised the terrible truth.

The tale of Henry Hash
Ended with a bash.
What could make a fat boy thin?
His sister joked,
His brother croaked,
As they popped him with a pin.

Heather Manger (12)
The Priory School, Shrewsbury

Zoo Animals

Why don't you let me free?
That's all I want to be,
Not locked up in a cage alone,
Nothing to do, nothing to see,
Just people banging on the glass laughing at me.
Leave me alone,
Locked up in a cage,
Why don't you let me free?
That's all I want to be,
Just free!

Hannah Gorski (12)
The Priory School, Shrewsbury

Battle Of Britain

On 16 July 1940,
The Luftwaffe attacked the RAF,
In a battle which was devastating,
For the pilots were plagued with death.

The operation Sea Lion,
Was a part of a destructive plan,
To take over Europe
Being led by one cruel man.

The German planes took to the air,
Setting them on a spree,
To kill all British planes,
And set the German strike free.

The 'Eagle Day' came,
With the Germans taking flight,
The British detected them with radar,
Whilst keeping out of sight.

The aircraft were outnumbered,
By about four to one,
Yet they took them by surprise,
For they were not yet done.

The Germans continued with their raids,
But lost six hundred planes,
As the RAF carried on killing,
The Luftwaffe were losing the reins.

Hitler ordered to attack the cities,
In a new tactical plan,
Expecting the British to surrender,
Fighting as hard as they can.

They may have been outnumbered,
But they battled to the last,
All the men who lost their lives,
Will never be forgotten in the past.

Will Jones (13)
The Priory School, Shrewsbury

A Young Girl's Weep

The wind was howling outside her room
As the little old lady
Awaited her doom.

As she lay in her bed
She listened to the sound of her daughter
Who had never been found.

Her eyes became heavy and her vision blurred
As she listened to her daughter
Who longed to be heard.

Just as she was drifting off to sleep
She heard the sound of faint footsteps
And a young girl's weep.

She sat straight up
Her face white as a ghost
As she realised it was the thing
That she feared most.

She picked up a candle
And walked across the floor
She slowly but carefully
Opened the door.

There was nothing there
So she shook her head
And with a sigh of relief
She walked back to bed.

As she turned to the wall
There was a sudden chill
As the words written were
'You're mine to kill . . .'

Suzy Marrs (13)
The Priory School, Shrewsbury

The Foot And Mouth Crisis

Foot and mouth was such a disaster,
But was it also a crime?
So many innocent lives were lost,
At such an awful time.

The farmers, they were hit hard,
With such a gigantic shock,
Most couldn't bear to see their cows,
And all of their poor, dead flock.

In came the men in white coats,
With shotguns at their side,
Farms were disinfected,
Lost was all their pride.

Huge fires, they were burning,
Of the animals all around,
Most hadn't even caught the disease,
But were buried underground.

Billions and billions of pounds were lost,
Over the space of two years,
The markets were deserted,
As the farmers faced their fears.

I know the country's still in shock,
About all the animals lost,
Most were killed for no reason at all,
And all for such a high cost.

Amy Wyatt (12)
The Priory School, Shrewsbury

Seaside

The blazing sun scorching my back,
The gentle ripple of waves,
Crabs scurrying around the sand,
Scuttling to their underground caves,
Like a deep mirror reflecting the sky,
With so many tones and shades,
The sea shows a clear sun,
Which into the distance fades,
Waves grasp out onto the sand,
Like hands scrabbling around,
The shrill, sharp squawk of seagulls,
Is among the seaside sounds,
The bright blue sky above me,
Changes from blue to red,
Orange and yellow entwines the clouds,
That surround me overhead,
Soon the stars are twinkling
The sea turns an angry black,
Thrashing around with tantrum,
The sky lights up with a crack,
A flash of lightning and the sea churns,
The whistling wind calls,
Maybe the sea isn't as friendly,
As I thought after all . . .

Sana Ayub (11)
The Priory School, Shrewsbury

Set Chickens Free!

Set chickens free,
They shouldn't be treated like trees.
In battery farms they're killed one by one,
Until there's finally none.

Or this would be if chickens aren't sent in every day,
To wait to be electrocuted in such a horrid way.
They wait in tiny cages all squashed together with barely room for air,
They struggle for food and water, this can hardly be called fair.

And who supports this horrible act which kills and tortures thousands of birds a day?
Why KFC and Burger King, who say to this OK.
Making millions off suffering and this makes cash registers ring,
Because they don't care a bit about this thing.

So don't eat battery-farmed chicken cos it'll only make you sick,
Even if you only have a lick.
This is horrible don't you agree?
So help set the chickens free!

James Fisher (12)
The Priory School, Shrewsbury

The Headache

It feels as though something is digging into my head,
trying to break into my brain!

It is something that sticks there for hours,
sabotaging anything I do, it's always there.

It inflicts pain in my head when I do anything,
I wish it would just drift away and leave me in peace,
but still it sips upon the blood of my pain.

It makes me feel depressed
and makes me dread wanting to do anything.

When it finally leaves me alone, my brain in malicious knots,
all my put-off work comes back to haunt me . . .

Fred Woollaston (11)
The Priory School, Shrewsbury

Bombs Go Bang

B rave
O rdinary
M en
B eing
S oldiers

G o
O ut

B rilliant
A nd
N everendingly
G lorious.

They will never leave us but remember . . .
'The old lie: Dulce et Decorum est Pro Patria Mori.'

With apologies to Wilfred Owen, 1893-1918.

Emma Neen (13)
The Priory School, Shrewsbury

I'd Like To Know
(Inspired by 'A Boy Called It' by David Pelzer)

Every day I love him but every day there's pain
The way he's treating me is driving me insane
It's not my fault she's not here
But every time he touches his beer . . .
He hits me.

She died when I was one
But the pain has never gone
I don't know what I've done
Remember I'm still your son
Why do you hate me so?
Because, Dad, I'd like to know.

Rosemary Evans (13)
The Priory School, Shrewsbury

My New Pet

The pet shop is now two miles away -
I am overwhelmed: at last I have a pet.
The responsibility will be mine,
I will have something of my own to love and care for at last.

Eventually the pet shop is in sight.
The cage is set up ready, a big change for the pet.
I hope some adventurous animal will soon be ours,
Looking for the most curious; boy or girl?

We ask to handle a few,
To see how the soft, silky scruff will react.
They scurry over my hand, so many colours,
Trying to nibble their possible owner.

In its cardboard box,
Its beady eyes look through at me.
I am eager to get this black-banded ball home,
To see the personality so I can name my pet.

Names go through my head,
As it spins, burrows and claws cling on the wires,
It strips sunflower seeds to the core.
In its teddy bear position it gives whisker kisses.

I decide to call my hamster 'Dusty'
Because of her colour and more.
She plays in the sawdust continually;
And shakes it off again.

We've got her home, I love her . . .
She seems so content,
I hope everything goes to plan. Will I cope?
The pet shop is two miles away.

Rachel Meyrick (12)
The Priory School, Shrewsbury

A Hero At War

It is really hurting,
But I must go on,
It is really hurting,
But my duty must be done.

All I feel is pain,
Got to keep on fighting,
All I feel is pain,
I wish this wasn't so frightening.

All I hear is shouting,
I can't stop this confusion,
All I hear is shouting,
And with feelings of delusion.

All I see is blurred,
Men scream and yell in pain,
All I see is blurred,
I hope this is not in vain.

All I feel is determination,
I feel this must be ending,
All I feel is determination,
How long can I keep defending?

Suddenly . . .

All I see are bodies,
Of those that I once knew,
All I see are bodies,
As their souls to Heaven flew.

All I hear is silence,
My fears have all gone,
All I hear is silence,
My duty here is done!

Lucy Jennings (12)
The Priory School, Shrewsbury

Diving In

There's the boy, the boy I see
I see him looking at me.

Will he ask me or shall I ask him?
I only see him when we swim.

He finally came up and asked me out
I was delighted, excited, I wanted to shout.

Our relationship was becoming steady
But then he was pushy, I wasn't ready.

He doesn't understand the way I feel
Surely this cannot be real.

We gave each other time and space
I don't want this to be a race.

As the weeks went by I wanted him near
Night after night I shed a tear.

Then one day whilst lunching a while
In he walks with the broadest smile.

We talked and talked and talked it through
Then we knew what we wanted to do.

He walked me home at the end of the night
He stood at my door and held me tight.

I ran inside to tell my mum
'Be equal,' she said, 'and go and have fun.'

I ran to him then with joy in my heart
Now is the time for our future to start.

Nikki Allcock (13)
The Priory School, Shrewsbury

Harry Potter Wizardry

I can make magic,
I can make spells.
Wizardry is my game,
Can't you tell?

I know plenty of witches,
Who have lots of riches.
I've seen frogs and owls,
And heard dogs that howl.

I can make magic,
I can make spells.
Wizardry is my game,
Can't you tell?

My history is mysterious,
With my parents dying out.
But I'm rather mischievous!
That goes without a doubt.

I can make magic,
I can make spells.
Wizardry is my game,
Can't you tell?

Shadows in the night,
With mystical creatures.
And a magical castle,
That has haunted features.

So what if I can do magic?
So what if I can do spells?
So what if my game is wizardry?
I know you can tell!

Hannah Wilson (15)
The Priory School, Shrewsbury

Friends And Acquaintances

There are many types of people, some large, some small,
There are many types of friends, some stay while others fall,
These allies can be true or may just want your help,
But only the whole friends can be decided by
If they come when you yelp.

We all have acquaintances but friends are harder to find,
It's good to have one or two because they may save your hind,
The world's a big place and even bigger without your friends,
If you don't have them then loneliness will never end.

Even the most evil things to ever walk the land,
Have been known to have a friend or two at hand,
Think about Hitler or bin Laden himself,
Without their mates they would have gone straight to the shelf.

Back in the old days when good old God was young,
He was Satan's pal and they had lot of fun,
But Satan was only an acquaintance, not a real friend,
He showed his true colours and to Hell he was sent.

Another instance is the old pirate days,
They said, 'Ahoy, matey,' because friendship pays,
You don't hear old Long John saying, 'Hello, acquaintance,'
If anyone did they'd need serious maintenance.

So, basically, it's always good to have a friend around,
Whatever the case, pals *must* be found,
Friendship has helped people all over the place,
You can be a pen pal and never see their face.

The world would be a sad place if we didn't have mates,
No one to throw up on at summer fêtes,
When your pet dies or your granny passes away,
You need a good cry and a friend, whatever the day.

If you're on a desert island in the middle of the sea,
You should have a friend there, no matter what the fee,
They can help you build shelter and gather some more food,
But at the end of the day they're just your best dude.

If you move schools or live somewhere new,
Keep your old pals but also make a few,
You should never forget how good your old ones are,
But make some others and they should stick like tar.
So I guess the message is basically this,
Pals can have fights, it won't always be bliss,
But a little effort can go a long way,
Make proper mates and friendships will stay.

Gareth Thomas (16)
The Priory School, Shrewsbury

A Hallowe'en Tale

Down the drive, the dark, long drive
Is a castle where no one lives and nothing can thrive
It's quiet and creepy, dismal and grey
A place where no one ever wishes to stay.

The floorboards creak and the bats fly free
The spiders' webs stream everywhere you can see
The grey rats scurry, hunting for food
While the raven in her nest is feeding her brood.

A tunnel of light from a cracked window on high
But still in the darkness we can't see the sky
A gust of wind sweeps past my feet
My blood turns cold, my heart misses a beat.

For the presence I feel is not only mine
The dust has unsettled, fingers run down my spine
Oh no, I must go and make my escape
And get away from this unheavenly place.

I turn and run and leave the shadows behind
Not even my freshly-made footprints you'd find
The only sound is my heart pounding with fear
As the castle grows distant and my safe home grows near.

Chloe Fletcher (12)
The Priory School, Shrewsbury

Witch War

I am a witch
And I am a girl
My family is dead
How will I be fed?
And with the witch in me
Be full of glee with the death of me?
Have I the power to fight
The evil's blight?
Or will evil succeed
And I be but a seed
To fuel
The evil's rule
And bring death to the ones I love?
Or will a glove
Hide the witch in me
So I can kill the evil Lord with glee?

James Holmes (15)
The Priory School, Shrewsbury

A Poem
(Inspired by the book 'Eagle Strike')

Fourteen,
Orphaned,
A reluctant MI6 agent.
Alex is no ordinary boy.
His life is full of violence and mystery.
Lonely, but never bored.
Short on family and friends,
He must sort out his own action-packed life,
In the style of James Bond.
Daring and eager to solve his tasks.
He even jumped from a sixth-storey window,
Just out of curiosity.

Chris Barber (13)
The Priory School, Shrewsbury

I Think I'll Just Curl Up And Die

I can't understand the world,
Think nothing - that's safest,
I'll be alright - will I?
Justice, where is it?
Curl me around your little finger,
Uphold some principles at least,
And let me in.
Die - when? Does it matter?
I think I'll just curl up and die.

Laura - Mother!
Why take a lover?
Am I not enough - for love?
Two new strangers in my life,
Him and . . . another!
Think - why don't you?

I can't understand the world,
Think nothing - that's safest,
I'll be alright - will I?
Think nothing - that's safest,

Let me in.

I think I will just curl up and die,
No! Think, think, think nothing!
Just *die*.

Sarah Lee (15)
The Priory School, Shrewsbury

Untitled

In his hand he holds his sword
All the protection he can afford
He brings it down sure and swift
His talent is his tribal gift
His final goal is now in sight
He swings again with all his might
But it's over now, he's won the fight.

Rachael Randall (15)
The Priory School, Shrewsbury

Poem Inspired By Malorie Blackman's 'Noughts And Crosses'

I stand and wait
Wait with my baby
Your baby
Our baby.

Watching
Watching and waiting
For you to come
Out, those two black, swinging injustices
With your head held high.

Time stands still
Still as the great steel-capped mountain
An endless seasonal stretch
North to south
Great wooden pillars
Towering above you
Scaffold
Rope
Trapdoor
Hands enchained
Your sorry world
Plunged into darkness
Swirling round in a beautiful, cascading waterfall
Pouring out the windows to your soul.

A crime you didn't commit
Unless true love
This beauty is a crime
Noughts and crosses
Never to be together.

You drop
A pearl lost to the roaring ocean
Swinging gently on the breeze
As it carries you away
Where some day we can be together.

I love you . . .

Claire Doyle (15)
The Priory School, Shrewsbury

Revenge Of The Chickens

Wendy the chicken, she really loves flowers,
She would just stare at them for hours and hours,
But Wendy the chicken went out one day,
To water the flowers, and have a short play,
She fainted with shock, and fell on the ground,
For flowers were being pulled up all around!
As she awoke, from this horrible dream,
She saw a sick sight too evil to be seen!
For although now the grass was more short and more clean,
The flowers were dead from a mowing machine!
Wendy decided that she'd make a vow,
To avenge those poor flowers, repay them somehow.
So on plodded Wendy through the eerie, still night,
And out jumped a figure, and Wendy took fright!
She assaulted the figure, and suddenly, then,
The figure cried, 'Help! Kindly spare a poor hen!'
So Wendy, she stopped, and looked on with shame,
As out of the darkness, a pretty hen came!
As Wendy waited, the chicken exclaimed,
'I'm Buttercup Primrose, flower lover by name!'
After a chat, the two became pally,
And quickly decided that they would be allies!
The two trotted off down the well-trodden path,
And they finally found the mower at last!
BP and Wendy gave small, evil grins,
And over the mower, they emptied vile bins!
Now the two felt quite sure that no grass would be mowed,
And quite happily, some new flowers they sowed!
The moral: though the two found the going quite tough,
You'll get what you want if you fight hard enough!

Becky Taylor (12)
The Priory School, Shrewsbury

Writing A Poem About Stephen King's 'Misery'

Paul Sheldon lies in a hotel room
Typing
About Misery Chastain
As she crawls to the end of
Her nurse's friend's life.

Adam Redman sits down in his bedroom
Scribbling
And reading in vain about Misery Chastain
As he
And his twin brother's friend
Consider similarities
And roots for a poem.

What Steve and Charlie and I
All know
Is that the space on the page
Is gone
To be filled up with further, continuing
Adventures
Of Paul and Misery
And Annie, her writer.

Adam Redman (15)
The Priory School, Shrewsbury

The Beach

As dusty as an attic,
As cheerful as a toy,
As sunny as the sun can be,
A playground full of joy.

The sea as cold as winter,
The sand as soft as snow,
At night the moon shines brightly,
The sky begins to glow.

Lucy Balcombe (13)
The Priory School, Shrewsbury

There's A Boy In The Girls' Dorm

There's a boy in the girls' dorm,
Like a predator looking for prey.
Pretending not to be born,
Hide away for the rest of that day.

There's a boy in the girls' dorm,
Out the window quick,
See him in his underwear,
I think I'm gonna be sick.

There's a boy in girls' dorm,
Mum is gonna go mad,
The teacher can't come in right now,
Nor can Hattie Yad!

There's a boy in the girls' dorm,
Share your sweets galore,
I think he is in Sarah's form,
Him and Claire kissing that is what I saw.

There's a boy in the girls' dorm,
End of all that fun,
There's a boy in detention,
Good luck, Calvin Clun.

Emma Lea (12)
The Priory School, Shrewsbury

My Dad's A Gorilla!

My dad's a gorilla when he gets mad,
He starts to rant and roar.
Then he walks about on his hands and knees,
And rolls all around on the floor.
He's also really hairy,
Hairs poke out his nose and through his vest,
And when he's really, really mad,
He stands and thumps his chest.

Becki Crawford (13)
The Priory School, Shrewsbury

So Powerful A Mere Picture
(Based on 'The House on the Strand' originally written by Daphne de Maurier)

All that I agree for
This had better be good
Vita will be along in a minute
Where have you taken me?
Take a trip down Magnus Lane and it always ends the same
When something I'll never see in the papers happens before my eyes.

Floating on the surface of a snowstorm
The glass will never break
And I will never find myself in that snow
Not that, there
I am frozen in the wasteland today
And I can't go back.

The numbness; the sweat can't stop me
You and the boys can't keep me from where I want to go
The guinea pig wants more than an effect.

Did you ever dream of going for a walk and all the lights are gone; and all the metal is gone?
Look under every stone
Look behind every tree
You'll never see it until it reaches and touches you
With its finger of death
Stalking you all the way since you left your home
So powerful a mere picture
Why, why, why did you trip on your way to dinner?

Edward Trethowan (15)
The Priory School, Shrewsbury

Corridor

Lying awake in the middle of night,
Trying to find the dream that's right,
Searching through the astral plane,
To find a place where knowledge I can gain.

Then, I speed through underground,
Trying to make sense of every sound,
Wondering where my destiny,
Take its energy and decide to take me.

Carpet slipping under feet,
Waiting to stop to take a seat,
But in my conscience it seemed best,
To keep walking without a rest.

Just when this was a bore,
I came upon an ancient door,
I reach forward to turn the knob,
Hoping now to finish the job.

I entered a room, taken aback,
I could see nothing, it was pitch-black,
Suddenly, a shout arose,
And I woke from my unusual doze.

I sat up and rubbed my eyes,
I felt like I had missed a big surprise,
Then, I fell straight back into slumber deep,
Hoping that I find the dream in my sleep.

Robert Pritchard (16)
The Priory School, Shrewsbury

Intimidation

So there she stands -
Giggling, gruesome with her friends;
Behind high-held hands
Whispered words waft my way, the ends
Of catty conversation touch my mind -
Unkind!
The feeling of attack,
When sniggering chimps chatter
Point and sneer behind my back!
I'm angry as I know it should not matter
But I'm powerless to reply . . .
I cry
But only in private;
Above all, *they* shall not see
The wounded me.
And I see no disgrace
In saying what you think to someone's *face*:
But can I go and look her in the eye?
(Or chest, as she towers ten feet high!)
One day I will -
When I am pushed too far
I'll turn the tide, I'll make my choice
I'll make my stand, I'll be the voice
For all the meek, pushed, shoved, cheated, sneered-at we
I'll stand up
And she'll meet the real me.

Tori Pearson (11)
The Priory School, Shrewsbury

Troy

The face that launched a thousand ships
Her beauty was worldwide
Paris eloped with Helen
A dagger at his side.

Menelaus, king of Sparta
With army to attack
Across the sea to Anatolia
To bring fair Helen back.

Troy, a city ten years under siege
The gates were fastened tight
The Greeks left the gift of the wooden horse
And disappeared into the night.

Greeks emerge from the horse
Once inside the walls
A Trojan arrow from Paris' bow
And noble Achilles falls.

Yet the Greek's triumphant army
Raze the city to the ground
Hell fire, death, destruction
Helen, the beauty is found.

Restored to Menelaus
Helen travels to her long-lost home
As wife to king of Sparta
The queen, no more to roam.

Olivia Hewings (13)
The Priory School, Shrewsbury

Jaded Education, Bizarrely Spent Leisure

Today I am telling him straight.
I am fed up with his obsession with me.
He believes he is my god; it just isn't normal.
The sun climbs into the blank sky,
Painting the city passionate orange.

The recited lines from Shakespeare are mis-said.
I would only smile if I thought there was good intent,
But he seems to hold a unique world of his own,
Where he is the talented sun
And commands the laws and language. I sigh uneasily.

This is the day that I change his dreary, malfunctioning world.
If he gives me half the chance to portray my vivid ideas,
I won't upset him; he already has so little in his dull life;
Just a skinny, scrawny cat curled up in a rented flat.

I walk the bustling street of the market;
Colourful garments screaming to be bought,
People making their way in the world.
And then I see him engrossed in his deadly silence,
His eyes dark like the devious night,
Signing on for his promised money.

No menacing grin, or sinful stare, purely nothing.
I drown in his deep, round pools of murky grey, suffocating.
My salty tears sting my wound,
But refuse to wash away my fresh blood.
Suddenly his eyes glitter. He can't touch me now.

Maya Garrett (14)
The Priory School, Shrewsbury

Seasons

When autumn leaves fall
It makes ponies drool
At the sight of a good old roll
They roll through and through
Till they've rolled up all.

When wintertime comes
And the pony is in its stall
The tongue pokes out to see what's about
And gets a mouthful of snow
That's how they know which season it is.

When springtime comes
They play in the rich, green grass
And the foals arrive at last
And dams whinny with joy
That's when they know spring has come.

When summertime comes
They bask in the midday sun
It's too hot to run
So they rest in the shade
Waiting till the good, cold days.

Becky Seward (12)
The Priory School, Shrewsbury

Today, I'm Going Away
(Based on Carol Ann Duffy's 'Education For Leisure')

Today, I'm going away, anywhere
I need to get away from him
His obsession is too great
One last walk around the town.

I struggled to break free of him
And I fear he is chasing me
He cannot understand my language
I must go.

I am not perfect
Though he fails to see that
He worshipped the ground I walked on
Too soon the bells he asked for.

He has become a monster, not the man I once knew
Rage has become him
He is everything evil personified
I start to speed up, he touched my arm . . .

Michael Beeston (14)
The Priory School, Shrewsbury

Sleepovers

S leeping over is such fun
L ying around and not looking glum
E veryone is invited in
E verything is to be put in the bin
P eople come and have lots of food
O f course everyone comes looking good
V ery soon we will have to go home
E veryone gets in the tent shaped like a dome
R un around and jump and shout
S cream and skip, now *get out!*

Laura Davies (13)
The Priory School, Shrewsbury

All Alone

I was always an outsider,
With almost no one around me,
No one to love me,
No one to care,
I just felt so alone.

And then the two people I trusted most,
Just left me out to die,
I didn't know where to go,
Who should I turn to?
I wished that I could just disappear.

Then something happened,
I honestly couldn't believe,
Strangers took me in and treated me with grace,
They helped me greatly,
In all that I did,
And life went well since then!

Sarah Cox (14)
The Priory School, Shrewsbury

Friends Forever

I'll always be here for you;
When you're sad,
As a shoulder to cry on.
When you're happy,
For a secret to share.
When you're cross,
To bring a smile to your face.
And when you're upset,
As an ear to listen.

I'll always be here for you,
As you are for me,
And hopefully ever shall be;
Friends forever!

Ciara Merrick (13)
The Priory School, Shrewsbury

The One That Got Away

From the killings I had done
Most I did without a gun
Pulling back their necks with force
Until for them, life was a closed door.

Spying had been our main aim
Preventing our enemy from enjoying further gain
Disaster struck when our cover was blown
And hence our position became known.

Times were desperate as we took flight
Only making progress through the night
Our ranks were thinned by the noise of rotor blades
The situation becoming increasingly grave.

Temperatures plummeted; the air seemed to freeze
We lost Vince, followed by our sense of ease
Hopes arise when a man offers aid
But it's a trick, Stan is taken, my escape will have to be self-made.

For days I struggled on alone
Until I found sanctuary in a kind family's home
Plying them with my store of gold coins
My route to freedom was finally joined.

I thought of my family and felt my heart full of love
I placed my trust and gave it all to up above
I looked up and gave Him a nod
Now I want to say, 'Thank you, God.'

Eloise Jackson (13)
The Priory School, Shrewsbury

Face

One moment in time,
Yet, just a few seconds.
It changed everything,
Changed one boy's life.

Martin, popular and pretty,
Smart and witty.
Went from everything to nothing,
Hero to zero.

A crash in a car
Smashed his face
Like Cobain's guitar,
Leaving him with a nasty case.

But would his friends stay by him?
Help him?
See him through till the end?

See, the human race is a funny thing,
Like a game and no one knows nuffin'!

Do we see people deep down?
Or do we judge people and wear a frown?

Mia Tivey (13)
The Priory School, Shrewsbury

Circus For One Night Only
(Inspired by 'Cirque Du Freak' by Darren Shan)

One fine afternoon in the schoolyard,
Four friends found a piece of paper,
As soon as they saw, they wanted more,
Of the curious promises made.

Only two tickets between the four,
They argued and quarrelled all day,
Lady Luck will choose, the other two lose,
A chilling adventure begins.

They take their seats and watch in awe,
As these freaks of nature perform for all,
The plot twists and turns as my stomach churns,
Darren's eyes are on the vampire's spider.

Darren returned and stole the spider,
To control it he played the flute,
He brought his friend round, then disaster abounds,
As the arachnid bit the friend.

Paralysis set in, a bargain was struck,
The friend's life for Darren's assistance,
An agreement was made, as the friend was saved,
Darren was now a half-vampire.

Neal Tomlinson (14)
The Priory School, Shrewsbury

Girl In Red

The long red skirt
Swayed in the wind,
As she walked past the light
He stared
At her pale plaits
As they swung side to side.
The harsh wind slashed his face
But yet
He carried on staring
At the magical gypsy that walked by.
She turned and stared,
They were in love
But they could never be together.
They didn't speak the same
But their thoughts brought them closer together.
Violent screaming
Broke the silence.
Police sirens screamed.
Although the girl in red didn't understand
She knew it was the sound of terror.
Tears stained her face
As her family was forced to move.
They knew they would be together
Someday
Somehow.

Amy Templeton (13)
The Priory School, Shrewsbury

The Curious Incident . . .

Why does no one understand?
Why do they make those silly demands?
I do not wish to kiss and hug,
When they do I will pull and tug.
Why am I expected to pay attention
When I am not addressed? How can I know I'm mentioned?
Why is it only me that sees so much?
I see the numbers but I don't like touch.

One night, what do I find but a dead dog.
A pitchfork straight in it, I see through the fog.
Mrs Shears finds me with her poodle deceased,
The police are called, I'm happy not in the least.

Why does no one understand?
Why do they make those silly demands?
I do not wish to kiss and hug,
When they do I will pull and tug.
Why am I expected to pay attention
When I am not addressed? How can I know I'm mentioned?
Why is it only me that sees so much?
I see the numbers but I don't like touch.

A tale unfolds, my mother returns from the grave,
I feel like I've been hit by a tidal wave.
And still the late dog Wellington stays on my m kind,
I decided to become an inspector of a kind.
I reveal the culprit - my own father it seems,
I find I share a murderer's genes.

Why does no one understand?
Why do they make those silly demands?
I do not wish to kiss and hug,
When they do I will pull and tug.
Why am I expected to pay attention
When I am not addressed? How can I know I'm mentioned?
Why is it only me that sees so much?
I see the numbers but I don't like touch.

I can't face talking to the man that has raised me for years,
But at least now I know the feeling of eyes full of tears.

Emma Jane Harris (13)
The Priory School, Shrewsbury

The Teenage Years

Where to start,
When do we change?
On the fatal day,
When we turn that age.

One minute we're nice,
And we're acting all normal.
Like any twelve-year-old child,
Just nice,
Not harmful!

When the clock strikes twelve,
On that decisive day,
We're only one year older,
Have we changed in any way?

The answer is yes,
What a difference it makes,
Our life from now on,
Is one massive mistake.

Like a poisonous snake,
I would advise *you* to stay away,
The chances we're in a good mood,
Is absolutely no way.

So much to think about now,
That we didn't have before.
Our hair, clothes and make-up,
When you're thirteen,
It's like a law.

The teenage years are deadly,
They're cruel and they're mean,
But, parents, these are nothing,
Compared to when we turn eighteen!

Becky Bruce (13)
The Priory School, Shrewsbury

Life . . .
(Based on 'Chinese Cinderella' by Adeline Yen Mah))

Life is sad,
Life can be bad.
But I will always know,
That one day I will glow.

The unwanted girl,
The despised sister,
Will one day find,
People will miss her!

Life is sad,
Life can be bad.
But she will always know,
That one day she will glow.

The mistreated boy,
The hated son,
One day he will show,
That his day has come!

Life is sad,
Life can be bad.
But he will always know,
That one day he will glow.

So you've had a bad time,
But now life's just fine.
So now everyone knows,
That every day your heart glows!

Alex Drake-Wilson (13)
The Priory School, Shrewsbury

PS: I Love You

It's never too late to say this phrase,
Even after many nights and days.
You can even say it in different ways,
But the best way is 'I love you'.

When you fall in love for the very first time,
Your heart is a bell you long to chime,
It even wants to make you rhyme(!)
But all you have to say is 'I love you'.

But beware, the results can be obscene,
When you say the words you do not mean,
To the one you like, but are not so keen,
Don't bother with 'I love you'.

After couples feel their love has died,
They've argued, bitched and even cried,
But one thing that they hadn't tried,
Was reminding them that 'I love you'.

From even the dead it still lives on,
When even the person you love's long gone,
And you feel as if you're all alone,
You can still say, 'I love you'.

Ellie Quinlan (14)
The Priory School, Shrewsbury

The X-Files

Mulder and Scully here they come,
Both grasping an automatic laser gun.
The dynamic pair never feared,
An extraterrestrial with a beard.

They always had an open mind,
To those who were not of a human kind.
Mad aliens and UFOs,
Always kept them on their toes.

Seeking out the adult victims dead,
While their children cry silently in bed.
A stab through the heart, a bullet to the brain,
While the blood pours out in the freezing rain.

Cloning is a hard to detect sin,
No idea which is the true kin.
Secret agencies and their lairs,
With secret agents to give aliens the scares.

A pair of girls set apart in different homes,
Both sharing the same genetic chromosomes.
FBI and MI6 keeping secrets bit by bit,
Each judging where the last piece of the puzzle should fit.

Mulder and Scully here they come,
Both with their trusty automatic laser gun.

Andrew Chebsey (13)
The Priory School, Shrewsbury

Burger Bar

I can't believe I've got to work at the burger bar,
Just so I can afford that brand new car.
I don't wanna work here, but I really need that money,
Everybody's got a car but me, do they think it's funny?
I can't believe I've got to work at the burger bar,
Just so I can afford that brand new car.
I walk in, but it smells bad so I walk straight out,
Try to consider my options but I realise there's nowt,
I can't believe I've got to work at the burger bar,
Just so I can afford that brand new car.
I walk back in, it's empty, a ghost town even,
Walk up to this man, the name badge says Steven,
I can't believe I've got to work at the burger bar,
Just so I can afford that brand new car.
He says go to see the manager in his room,
And when I walk in, that's when I realise I'm doomed.
2 weeks on, I'm bored as Hell,
I know I've got to quit, mainly because of the smell,
I can't believe I've got to work at the burger bar,
Just so I can afford that brand new car.
I walk out of the bar, I'm free, c'mon,
So what if I don't have a car? What if I'm the only one?
I'm not working at this burger bar,
I don't give a damn about that brand new car.

Tom Davies (13)
The Priory School, Shrewsbury

Luna And Toci

We set them free.
My heart full with happiness once again.
They loved it.
Running free on the plains.

They killed to fill their stomachs.
They kept each other warm.
They fought against threats in nightfall.
Life was perfect for them.
Together.

One night it smelt them.
One night it stalked them.
That night it killed one.

His brother first confused.
But now running wild and free.
Alone.

Jasmin Bayliss (15)
The Priory School, Shrewsbury

Looking In The Mirror!

Looking in the mirror
The reflection that I see
This ugly, moronic creature
Is looking right back at me.
A cluster of bright red puss balls
Some black dots thrown in too
Long, dark, greasy hair
And a mouth that's full of goo.
One day when I look in the mirror
A beautiful princess I hope to see
With shiny hair and perfect skin
And my ugly braces in the bin.

Camilla Clay (13)
The Priory School, Shrewsbury

Indigo Night

Indigo night with diamond stars
The war wages on, fierce like Mars
The big black dog fights the moon
If he won, it would be too soon.

The planes melt into poppies
Swaying in the breeze
The big black dog sniffs the flowers
The sniff of pollen makes him sneeze
The poppies swirl into colourful coral
The bees are turned into fish
As a shark comes along, disturbing the peace
The dog runs away, not wanting a death wish.

The sun pours in, like syrup on stone
And I'm woken up by the sound of the phone
My thoughts turn to breakfast, away from my dream
But my mind still wondering - *what does it mean?*

Ashleigh Bennett (13)
The Priory School, Shrewsbury

Answers

Imagine a world
A world without injustice
A world with no hate.

The calming waters;
A ripple on the surface
Disturbing the peace.

There are no answers;
Only questions in this world
Of lies and deceit.

Rachel Benson (14)
The Priory School, Shrewsbury

Why Is It Always Me?

Every day is always the same,
Taunts and jibes, continual pain,
A hit, a punch, a kick in the knee,
Why is it always me?

Is it because I'm too fat or too thin?
Nobody knows their reasoning.
Ugly or pretty I just can't see,
Why is it always me?

Constant taunting all day long,
Makes me feel I will never belong.
This time next year where will I be?
Why is it always me?

Why do I feel so alone?
My only help is on the phone.
How come nobody can see?
Why is it always me?

Georgina Minton (13)
The Priory School, Shrewsbury

The Toad

As Tommy walked down the winding road
He met a large, but friendly toad
It hopped right up to Tommy to greet
And jumped up at least 3 whopping feet.
It caught poor Tommy by surprise
Almost popped into his eyes.
With hands outstretched he touched the toad
What a slippery, slimy, fidgeting load.
It croaked at Tommy, who jumped in surprise
Scaring the creature almost as much as he.
So now friends they could not be
What had started out to be such fun
Had ended in a scary one.

Simon Stallard (13)
The Priory School, Shrewsbury

Cirque Du Freak

The Circus of Freaks,
A big top full of mutants,
The vivid Madame Octa,
Obeying the vampire's wish.

Now the show is over,
A vampire to be questioned,
Though only good blood needed,
To suck life from the living.

A spider spinning thoughts,
Which one man has possessed,
A musical web of silence,
Motionless by the wound.

A life or death decision,
A potion to revive,
Trading one spirit for another,
Rising nightly from the grave . . .

Emma Hunt (13)
The Priory School, Shrewsbury

Old People

Old people -
Old and withered, with their slippers on,
Sitting by the fire with a book.
Grandma Josephine and Grandad John,
Doing the wheelchair and walking stick look.
Some would say they're over the hill,
Pastimes are knitting and sleeping,
But how, for so long, can they sit so still?
You never know whether they're alive or dead,
Or whether they're dreaming in their head.

Madeline Watkins (13)
The Priory School, Shrewsbury

The Week Before Christmas

'Twas the week before Christmas and in each homely retreat,
Every family was watching 'Coronation Street'.
Meanwhile poor Santa tried hard to remember,
Just when was Christmas? Which day in December?
He went outside to feed all of the reindeer,
A flying concoction of flaked barley and beer.
To have any effect it took at least one full day,
So off he went to load up his sleigh.
Why did the children want such impossible things,
Like Orlando Bloom and ponies with wings?
When he mounted his sleigh many hours later,
He turned on the radio and satellite navigator.
Soaring out into the dark, night sky,
Hoping for 'milk' and a tasty mince pie.
The first stop he made was Hereford Road,
Where he hoped to lighten up his load.
But as he drew nearer, what could he see?
No, it most certainly could not possibly be!
Had he come on the wrong night?
Everyone was awake and everywhere was light.
Perhaps Santa could have avoided this mess up,
If only he'd been for his BUPA health check-up.
He was not a spring chicken anymore,
In fact, he was one thousand, two hundred and twenty-four.
Quickly he turned the reindeer back,
Only stopping at Pizza Hut for a speedy snack.

Rosanna Franklin (13)
The Priory School, Shrewsbury

All Alone

Lonely, upset and timid,
Sat in the corner.
All alone.
No friends,
No family,
Nothing.

Sad, depressed and scared,
Just her in the playground.
All alone.
No friends,
No family,
Nothing.

Vulnerable, unaware and blank,
She walked on the old trodden path.
All alone.
No friends,
No family,
Nothing.

Senseless, deaf and blind,
She hung from the rope in her room.
All alone.
No friends,
No family,
Nothing.

Apart from those whose hearts yearned for the girl,
Who hung herself in her room.
Her life was made,
A living Hell,
Thanks to a girl in her class.

Charlotte Harrison (14)
The Priory School, Shrewsbury

A Crown Of Swords
(Based on 'A Crown Of Swords' by Robert Jordan)

Charnel corpses litter the ground,
The butcher's yard indeed,
Forty-thousand souls pound
Upon the Dark One's door.

As the world stews,
Fools strive for position,
Forming into queues,
To be cut down on the last day.

The old enemy newly-discovered
Lays in wait in the city of darkness,
A trap uncovered,
Leads to final and eternal death.

All that is,
And all that was,
Balances on the edge of a knife.
The only certainty is that the end comes.

Christopher Shaw (16)
The Priory School, Shrewsbury

On Playing Nancy

Please, Sir, I'd like some more
I would not be breaking the law
So do not kick me out the door
Or beat me with a stick.

'Cause I am hungry, can't you see?
You haven't dished out enough for me
A full stomach would fill me with glee
So don't beat me with a stick.

Top hats and coats, you gentlemen
Would take pity on my hunger then
And give me extra nourishment
Not beat me with a stick.

Abby Quinlan (15)
The Priory School, Shrewsbury

The Valley

It is my place of peace,

Slowly making my way down to the floor.
The soft ground springy underneath my feet.
The usual sounds of city life ebbing away,
The light slowly getting dimmer.

As I get deeper

The valley floor is quiet, all except the sounds of the birds
And of running water.

There is a place under a tree,
Where the rays of light
Punch through the dense canopy around me
The green, flowing leaves rustling over my head.

The water of the stream,
Slowly, and gently running along the bottom of the valley.
The thin, golden rays of light bouncing off the water.

Moving out of the valley,
All anger and stress having leaked out of me,
And washed away by the slow ebb of the stream.

Out into the hustle and bustle of modern life.

Matt Harrison (14)
The Priory School, Shrewsbury

Wild And Free

Galloping wild through the wind,
As light as air and as graceful as a swan,
Making shadows as she passes,
Her silky mane shining as the sun glistens down,
The mane is flowing like the waves,
A flash of dark bay as she glides,
She looks just like a glittering gown.

Kaytie Evans-Jones (11)
The Priory School, Shrewsbury

Bridget Jones's Diary

Daniel Cleaver; office boss,
Ultimate sex god,
That he was.

Flirting over computers,
Couldn't believe my eyes,
Thought skirt was off sick,
Slowly learned he told me packs of lies.

Found him with naked American girl,
All cosy in his apartment,
My thoughts went in a whirl.

How could he have done this to me?
Why didn't he see
I was in love with him?
Wasn't he in love with me?

Phoned up Shazza, Tom and Jude,
Told them what happened,
They all supported me,
And said he was lewd.

Had a night out with Tom and Gav,
To the Saatchi Gallery for an art exhibition,
Saw Daniel at what looked to be the toilets,
He told me not to wee on the installation.

Eventually found the real toilets,
And broke down in tears,
Tom came to find me,
And took me home.

Tom told me Gav liked me,
He's only twenty-two,
Probably wouldn't like me now,
After I cried in the loo.

Amy Harrison (15)
The Priory School, Shrewsbury

New School!

The holidays have been and gone
There's a fluttering in my tum
I just don't know what lies ahead
As I say goodbye to Mum.

The walk up to the big front door
Seems to take a thousand years
My legs are jelly and my head
Is full of doubts and fears.

At secondary school
They think you're a fool
The teachers are cruel
Their tyrannical rule
Means you work like a mule
They feed you on gruel.

New shoes, new coat, new pencil case
New uniform, new book
Big new bag that weighs a ton
New work, new friends with luck.

And now I've been here for a month
And settled in quite well
I like big school but not as much
As the going home time bell.

At secondary school
You'll find as a rule
That everything's cool!

Alex O'Fee-Worth (11)
The Priory School, Shrewsbury

The Old Oak Tree

Hundreds of years old,
The oak tree stands,
Alone in a field,
With its forgotten past.

Memories of youth slowly fade,
When children swung on its branches,
Its leaves were green and flowers bloomed,
Now leaves are brown and frowning.

Proud it stood, long, brown arms,
Swaying with its brothers and sisters in a young boy's yard,
But to its surprise the house came down,
And with it his family, now he's alone.

Hundreds of years old,
The oak tree stands,
Alone in a field,
With its forgotten past.

Bethany Thomas (11)
The Priory School, Shrewsbury

The Lord Of The Night

Slowly, creeping, quiet as can be
The evil stalker of the night
Can be seen momentarily.

Darting this way
Then flashing back
Fierce as a dog
Stealthy like a cat.

The hunter, vicious
And full of fright
Ruler of darkness
Lord of the night!

Alex Emberton (11)
The Priory School, Shrewsbury

Countryside

The countryside is a peaceful place,
Factories and cars that look so small.
Animals and leaves move around,
Blackberry bushes, that's not all.

You can see meadows for miles and miles,
Beautiful views all around.
Valleys and hills everywhere,
There's hardly a sound.

I love the countryside,
Movement here and there.
Lovely place to have a picnic,
It's a nice place for me and you to share.

Megan Rose Reece (11)
The Priory School, Shrewsbury

The Countryside

The sun is shining in the sky
The grass is blowing in the breeze
I see birds flying high
I see the squirrels in the trees.

In the fields the lambs are playing
I hear the other children having fun
I also hear the horses neighing
I see a family having a picnic.

All around me are beautiful views
There are hills, meadows and valleys
We're lucky to have the countryside to use
We go down the muddy track, kicking leaves.

Rosie Coxhead (11)
The Priory School, Shrewsbury

Walking Through A Field

Gentle breeze following me,
Leaves swaying in the
Sunlight.
Dew still on the long
Strands of grass.
River trickling along
Beside me.

Step by step I'm seeing more,
It's beautiful and calm,
Peaceful and relaxing.
Cows munching on the dewy grass,
Horses running by the shady trees,
Fish leaping in and out of the water.

I come to the bridge,
I stop,
I can't stop staring,
I see the best thing in the world,
Another field.

Georgina Thomas (14)
The Priory School, Shrewsbury

Heaven

The evening breeze rippled through his hair.
The distant lights of the town
Twinkled far away.
The leaves on the trees swayed in the wind
And the moon shone brightly down.

The few remaining songbirds
Fluttered to their nests
And the musical chirrup
Slowly faded, carried off into the night
And all his worries drifted with them
Here in this paradise.

Matthew Edwards (11)
The Priory School, Shrewsbury

What Am I?

I'm tired of children running on me,
Playing ball and fighting on me,
I'm bored with hearing arguments here and there,
And then there are some who hurt themselves
And go weeping to the nurse.
Those kids don't seem to care about me,
And some don't even notice me!
And yet I give them a place to play,
But never have I heard thanks!
So, one day soon, when the bell's just rung,
And all the eyes are gone,
I'm going to pick myself up and run and run and run,
Out of that gate and down the road,
To find myself a retirement home!

Lucie Short (11)
The Priory School, Shrewsbury

The Seaside

When it's cold at night
And no one's about
I hear the waves
Jump and shout
A breeze in the air
A shout from the sea
In the sky was a moon
As bright as could be
The sand moved softly
Side to side
And the air spoke swiftly new
The owls started hooting in the trees above.
What a strange night it was too.

Melissa Amy Morris (11)
The Priory School, Shrewsbury

Secret Garden

I sit alone
Nothing but Mother Nature surrounds me
The sun's warm rays beating down, the morning
Frost twinkling like a glacier in the depth of the ocean.

A little red robin perches delicately on a branch above
Its gentle serenade filling the skies
Malted, golden leaves rustle as the brisk breeze whispers in my ear
Telling me untold secrets of passers-by
I listen vigilantly and giggle at the thought.

This is my place of thought
I reflect on days gone by
I even share my most inner thoughts with the breeze
It always listens to me and my voice.

I watch the flight of the birds
Encircling the sun
Oh how I do wish to be free!
Free to be able to go where I wish
Where I live no one cares about me or my life
I have never been loved
Those people don't even know what love means.

But here I am at one with the things I love
Nature loves me in return
A small tear trickles down my face like a gentle stream on a nice day
It makes a small splash on my worn-out jeans.

The breeze picks up, it encircles me
It sensed I was upset
It gives me a warming cuddle to lift my spirits
I close my eyes and just dream . . .

Hayley Steadman (14)
The Priory School, Shrewsbury

Waterfall Poem

I arrived at sunrise
Molten gold stained a pure black night
Birds' songs and cries filled the still sky
They silhouetted the big, round sun
They flew freely
I longed to fly with them; instead I walked on.

Around me once again it was silent
Peace seeped through the atmosphere
Only the rustling of an animal cracked the winter freeze
As the dew melted around my feet,
The glistening webs revealed,
The icicles from bracken drip
And the roaring of the roaring, growling of the waterfall
Took control.

I stood and watched in awe
As tumbling waves swallowed gentle trickles of purity
The frothing whips of waves lashed out,
They struck the ancient rocks of time,
As they stood strong.
These remembered times the water could not tell of
I waited until the day had dawned.

I walked away from the grasps of the
Waterfall.

Holly Ashford (14)
The Priory School, Shrewsbury

Bonfire Night

It's cold.
It's freezing, but exciting.
I can hear the excitement,
Rushing round the field.
The audience is waiting,
Waiting for the firework show to begin.
The fire's lit,
The cracking sound as it waves to everyone,
It shows off,
Flashing its eyes at the amazed people.
Bang!
Bang, bang!
The squeals and shouting racing through my head.
And I wonder,
I wonder where the rockets are going,
Before they explode,
And I'm daydreaming,
Losing myself,
As I watch a rocket glide towards me . . .

Bang!

Jennifer Smyth (11)
The Priory School, Shrewsbury

Seasons

When spring has sprung
And the worms are glum,
You can stand while sitting on the floor.
Swimming lambs around the fields,
Bright bulbs see the daffodils peeled,
By the light of the tartan boar.

When the summer snows are falling
And the young seaweed are calling,
Flying buckets eat sandcastles in the shade.
Sailing ice-green wafer crumpets,
Playing, smiling limestone trumpets,
Calling out to blistered bathers with a spade.

When autumn leaves you dreaming,
Eating conkers on the ceiling,
Woolly jumpers cycle bravely through the corn.
Falling apples start to chatter
With the branches full of batter,
Smoking bonfires leave the ripping grey sky torn.

When winter falls like cotton wool
And frozen fireflies start to pull
The icing from red plastic Christmas cakes,
Chilling rainbows span the heavy sky,
Black foggy boots, they melt and sigh
Until the New Year robin, oven bakes.

Danielle Dodd (11)
The Priory School, Shrewsbury